DRIFTING SKANDHAS

a Philosophical, Artistic and Literary Commentary on the Heart Sutra

Li Sen

Translated by
Deng Zhihui

Published in Australia by

Heart Space Publications

January 2022

Heart Space Publications
315 Kline Street, Ballarat East, Victoria, 3350, Australia
Tel +61 450260348
www.heartspacepublications.com
pat@heartspacepublications.com

First published in Chinese by
The Commercial Press, Ltd., Beijing, in 2018

With the title 《法蕴漂移》

Copyright © 李森 (LI Sen) 2018
English translation 邓志辉 (DENG Zhihui)

We thank the Chinese Fund for the Humanities and Social Sciences for their kind financial support of the publishing of this book.

All rights reserved under international copyright conventions.
No part of this book may be reproduced, stored in a retrieval system, or transmitted in any form or by any means electronic, mechanical, photocopying, recorded or otherwise without written permission from Heart Space Publications.

Whilst every care has been taken to check the accuracy of the information in this book, the publisher cannot be held responsible for any errors, omissions or originality.

Australian Publishing in January 2022 at Melbourne.

ISBN 9780648921677

Contents

Testimonial, by Dorian Haarhoff		v
Translator's Preface		1
Author's Preface		7
Chapter 1	Chanting and Knocking	5
Chapter 2	Call and Response	25
Chapter 3	A Hero Poem	7
Chapter 4	Dialogue and Enlightenment	49
Chapter 5	The Beauty of Vyaavalokayati	65
Chapter 6	The Language of Skandhas	75
Chapter 7	Emptiness is Wind	85
Chapter 8	The Prayer Wheel of Language	97
Chapter 9	All Dharmas are Empty	107
Chapter 10	Thus Have I Said	121
Chapter 11	The Way the Five Skandhas Exist	133
Chapter 12	Rupa-Skandha is the 'Line in the Magic Horn'	41
Chapter 13	The Tidal Force of Spiritual Liberation	153
Chapter 14	The Form–Emptiness Wheel	163
Chapter 15	Harmony within Skandhas of the Subjective Mind	175
Chapter 16	The Drifting and Turning of Skandhas	193
Chapter 17	Skandhas Adrift under Provisional Names	205
Chapter 18	An Unobstructed Mind	219
Chapter 19	The Twelve Links of Dependent Arising, the Four Noble Truths and 'That Person'	231
Chapter 20	Nirvana and the Mantra Flow	245
The Prajnaparamita Heart Sutra in Sanskrit (Transliteration)		259
The Prajnaparamita Heart Sutra in Chinese (Xuanzang translation)		263
The Prajnaparamita Heart Sutra in English (based on Red Pine translation)		265
Notes on The Prajnaparamita Heart Sutra		267
About the Author		285

Testimonial

Chanting may take the powerful course of surging rivers, rushing in all directions, or the leisurely flight of geese migrating across the sky, or the forceful pattern of stirring wind blowing over the earth.

Li Sen

Li Sen's *Drifting Skandhas* is a poetic testimony to an ancient practice essential to our life and times. Li Sen writes, 'I chant the *Heart Sutra* because it is a doorway of radiant emptiness opening into the soul. Yet this doorway has neither frame nor threshold.' This is akin to the doorway celebrated in many mystic traditions.

Here, an anecdote from the West attests to the power of chanting:

> In the late 1960s the monks in a French Benedictine monastery had grown lethargic. They were reluctant to stir their limbs to work in the vineyards. The new abbot called in a physician who checked out the men. He could not find anything amiss. Then the abbot called in a dietician who said, 'Perhaps the monks need a meat diet.' He put them on meat and they became even more lethargic. These Benedictines had been vegetarians for hundreds of years.
>
> Then the abbot called in a therapist who worked in a special way. The therapist sat down with the abbot and asked, 'You are new around here. What changes have you introduced?' 'Well', said the abbot, 'The monks used to chant three hours a day. In order to make them more productive in the vineyards, I removed chanting from their daily calendar.' The sound therapist, whose name was Dr Alfred Tomatis, urged, 'Put back the chanting.' The abbot did. In a short time the monks had regained their level of energy.

Chanting energises the brain. The word 'enchantment' comes from the same root. So does canto (cantare), meaning 'sing' in Latin. According to the Biblical tradition, 'In the beginning was the Word.' In Eastern traditions, in the beginning was sound. This book marries word and sound, for, as Li Sen states, 'Chanting is by nature a poetic practice devoid of depth structure, value judgement or historical burdens. The mind, deeply besieged by the material world and conceptual meanings, needs to take an urgent step to break down the walls that trap it, set sail on its pilgrimage toward ultimate liberty of life, and attain self-redemption.

We are offered a synthesis of academic, philosophic, anti-philosophic (Lacan), artistic, literary and poetic modes. The great Buddhist classic, the *Heart Sutra*, seeks to transcend the constraints of academicism. The walls between written forms are illusory. It is not argument that transports us through the paradoxically named Gateless Gate, where 'form is emptiness, emptiness is form', but the wings of imagery. The book can be considered an extended koan. Nor does it follow a linear path for it can be 'shuffled and randomised freely, with its poetic spirit totally unchanged'.

The text, like that of the ancient Chinese sage—poets, is rich with the author's poetry, in which metaphors take us as far as language can go before it touches silence and enters the inexpressible. Li Sen offers us a kaleidoscope of images, pointing to the insights that nature provides:

> *The cock crows, drinking in the remnants of the sun.*
> *The cock coos, drinking in fleeting time.*
> *Its crows are chained together like the peaks of mountains,*
> *as swarms of incipient rainclouds hanging in the sky.*

(Li Sen)

It is not always easy to understand. It requests our attention, and a focused reading, as we uncover the Buddhist view of the universe, in which the Five Skandhas, namely, form, sensation, perception, memory and consciousness, 'empty of self-existence', lead to evolving awareness. Li Sen's meditation on the Dharma, that is teachings of the Buddha, needs some unpacking for minds fed on duality. 'Buddhist philosophy...dancing between these various modes of being, is the...philosophical activity of a non-philosophy.'

Li Sen's insights become available to us through the poetic image, which belies any dogma or fixed interpretation. 'Skandhas are like flocks of geese that migrate across the sky, leaving the sky with only emptiness and the mind with only a faint shadow. They are the flocks of geese being "looked upon"; they are also the "looking" by the geese themselves. They are the wailing of a single goose in wilderness; they are also the waggling of flocks of geese across the sky.'

The notes of the interpretive and explanatory translator, Deng Zhihui, offer eyes and ears accustomed to English an entry point, a guide to Buddhist philosophy and culture, as in the observation, 'In Buddhism, bubbles and dreams are two commonly used metaphors for describing the illusory nature of existence. Other similar metaphors include a dewdrop, a phantom, a flash of lightning in a summer cloud, a flickering lamp'.

The text is repetitive, with a refrain, much as a chant invites a growing comprehension as the person chanting enters the flow of the river of the refrain: *'Gate gate, paragate, parasangate, bodhi svaha'*. This is comparable to the Western monastic tradition, where the practice of *Lectio Divina* entails a text being read three times, with each reading entering deeper into the mystery.

The book is wide-ranging in its allusion to complementary texts and authors: *Yi Jing* (or *Book of Changes*), *Dao De Jing* (or *Classic of the Way and Virtue*), Martin Heidegger, Ludwig Wittgenstein, Karen Armstrong and others. Bill Porter features frequently: 'A mantra is like a magic lamp. If you rub it correctly, its resident genie will appear. Mantra is a mystical formula of invocation. It has no specific semantic meaning, but that is precisely what makes it meaningful.' These accompanying figures pointing to the same mystery.

The abiding metaphor of drifting accompanies the author's exposition. His Language Drift Theory focuses on casting adrift the skandhas that have assembled in mind. The limitations of languages can capture only fragments of skandhas, which are but cloud-like 'phantasms'. In Li Sen's words, 'Language is not wind, but wind can be used as a metaphor to refer to language.'

Language can fetter us, as it masquerades as reality. In the drift of language, chantable rhythm exists not simply for revealing meaning or ideas, but to remind us of ever-changing nature. Such language, in which nouns like 'nirvana' and 'skandha' may morph into verbs, enables us to return to our own true nature.

Li Sen, in a bow to his mentors and sources, quotes the poet, Su Shi (1037–1101), on the secrets of writing. 'Not liable to set rules, a good piece of writing moves on freely and smoothly like floating clouds or flowing water. Clouds drift and form new skyscapes every other day; a good writer works out his excellence in relation to the material about which he is writing. Thus is created the natural unity and coherence of writing with rich spontaneous creativity.' This reflects Li Sen's practice. Such writing is 'not to be read as a narrative, but to be chanted as verse'.

Drifting Skandhas requests the reader to do what the poet David Whyte asks in his poem 'Tilicho Lake', set in Nepal:

> **In this high place
> it is as simple as this,
> leave everything you know behind.**

At a time of turmoil and Earth crisis, Heartspace Publications provides a complementary home for the English version of this elucidation of the Heart Sutra.

Dorian Haarhoff
2021, Pringe Bay, South Africa

Dr Dorian Haarhoff is a poet, mentor and speaker and a former professor of English literature (University of Namibia) who facilitates writing and story-telling wordshops.

Translator's Preface

I felt incredibly honoured, though slightly stressed, when the Chinese Fund for the Humanities and Social Sciences formally entrusted me with the translation of *Drifting Skandhas: A Philosophical, Artistic and Literary Commentary on the Heart Sutra*. By then, I had done a sample translation of the first several chapters, and so was entirely clear about the likely challenging nature of the task.

The challenge was two-fold: first, the understanding of Buddhist philosophy, which is a central theme of the book, and, secondly, the transference of the highly literary, figurative language that pervades the book.

Though Buddhism has played a significant role in shaping Chinese culture, most people, including me, have a comparatively superficial understanding and limited knowledge of it. Adding to the complexity of the situation, the author repeatedly emphasises that, Buddhism as a philosophy is different from Buddhism as a religion. If it is comparatively easy to translate Buddhist terms into English, it is much harder than expected to fully comprehend their true meanings, or the philosophy that underlies them. This may in turn cause trouble in understanding a seemingly straightforward sentence or paragraph. For this reason, I have read widely in the field, tracing the sources of Buddhist philosophical ideas, to ensure a better grasp of Buddhist teachings. In translating Buddhist terms, which may appear as various renderings in English, I have, after referring to multiple sources, on the whole followed the translations of Bill Porter (Red Pine), though not exclusively so. Readers may refer to the 'Notes on *The Prajnaparamita Heart Sutra*' at the end of the book for a detailed explanation of key Buddhist terms that appear in the *Heart Sutra* and in this book.

Given that this is essentially an academic work, I have also tried, where necessary, to help the reader bridge the information gap by providing footnotes explaining Buddhist, philosophical or cultural topics. In some cases, missing information is provided by judicious addition of a few phrases in the immediate context of the text.

Another challenge comes from the prevalent metaphorical expressions. The author generally writes in the succinct style of philosophical prose, but from time to time, the language becomes figurative, like that of poetry. This is not surprising, since the author is a practising poet apart from being a scholar. The poet in the scholar hopes to 'restructure the mind by reviving the poetic power that has been endowed, with dignity, to every human heart.' The creative, metaphorical language employed in his scholarly discussion, along with the many short poems that intersperse the text, can be seen as the poet's weapon to 'break through the walls of the mind, so that the flickering yet shining poetic spirit of rhetoric can drift across lands and travel far like spring winds'.[1]

In translating, I have striven to stay faithful to the author's aesthetic pursuit by preserving much of the original flavour of the Chinese, while avoiding a rigid literal translation, which would distort meaning by obscuring sense. This can, from time to time, cause the translation to read not quite like

---

[1] *Translator's Note*: See Author's Preface. The quotations in this paragraph are typical of the kind of metaphorical language employed by the author in the book.

native English, but the reader may, hopefully, catch a glimpse of another culture's patterns of thinking, and hear the literary voice of another language's rhythms and cadences. I dare not assert that I have succeeded in this, but it has certainly served as a guiding principle for my translation.

I would like to express my deep gratitude to Thomas Garbarini and Nick Rosenbaum, who undertook the job of translating most of the poems in the book. Both of them have rich experience of Chinese–English literary translation, and their wonderful translations of the poems certainly add lustre to the whole. Thomas Garbarini has translated most of the poems in chapters 1 to 12, while Nick Rosenbaum undertook most of those in chapters 13 to 20. The translator's name is noted under each poem. They have also been helpful in other ways in my own translation process: providing feedback, giving suggestions, or simply talking through confusing points with me. I feel extremely fortunate to have had them to refer to when complexities arose.

Sincere thanks also go to the following individuals. Professor Li Sen, the author of the book, has been kind and patient in explaining his intentions to help me understand his writing. Pat Grayson, my editor at Heartspace Publications, helped me improve the translation by giving invaluable feedback on various drafts. An Xiaohui, Jiang Shanshan and Li Yadi, from The Commercial Press (publisher of the book in Chinese), have all provided much assistance through the process. A most sincere thank-you to Sarah Waldram, whose professional, flawless editing and proofreading brought about tremendous improvement in style and clarity. It is only with the support of all the above-mentioned people that this work has been possible.

DENG Zhihui
December 25, 2020

Traveller on the Way.
Hanging scroll,
ink on paper, 108 × 29 cm,
by Dan Dang.

Author's Preface

Thus have I said:[2] this book seeks to interpret The *Prajnaparamita* Heart Sutra in light of the Language Drift Theory that I have proposed. To interpret is, in effect, to undergo a process of planting, as well as preserving, rhetoric in the boundless realm of the human heart. Or, to revive rhetoric, over and over again, by staying true to chuxin[3] (the open state of mind of a beginner) and thus enable it to break through the walls of the mind, so that the flickering yet shining poetic spirit of rhetoric can drift across lands and travel far like spring winds.

A glance at how language and symbols have been used or created in the fields of philosophy, art and literature, immediately reveals that an oversupply of concepts and ideas, through continuous production and reproduction, have piled up into heaps of academic waste, resulting in an unbearable shade and suppression of the mind. I have hence long wanted to restructure the mind by reviving the poetic power that has been endowed, with dignity, to every human heart.

---

2 *Translator's Note:* This is a coinage from 'Thus have I heard', which is a standard way of beginning a Buddhist sutra, normally rendered in Chinese as *rushiwowen* (如是我闻). The author clearly intends to bring *rushiwowen* to the reader's mind, though he changes *wen* ('heard') to *shuo* ('said'). He thus implies the close relationship between the following chapters and Buddhist teaching.

3 *Translator's Note:* Chuxin literally means 'a beginner's mind' or 'beginning mind'. In Buddhism, it refers to the state of mind when one first brings forth the Bodhi mind. This beginner's mind is awakened mind itself. Since a true beginner's mind is empty and ready for new things, chuxin is now widely used to refer to the idea of letting go of preconceptions, or to employ an attitude of openness.

Indeed, to plant or to preserve rhetoric is to call forth what has been endowed to the human heart and mind. For it is through the sound and form created by rhetoric that reality manages to manifest itself, just like stars manifesting themselves through the brilliance of light. The awakening of each piece of rhetoric opens possibilities of a revival of reality in the mind, with the reborn rhetoric in perfect tune with the newly gained conception, just like a melody played harmoniously on the strings of a harp.

When rhetoric is planted or preserved, it undergoes a dynamic process of travelling and drifting. This process of appropriating rhetoric for a fitting conceptualisation of objects, if it has any objective at all, is meant to enable the poetic quality of rhetoric to emerge, be highlighted and grow freely. In this respect, any activated or self-activated rhetoric is used as a verb rich with poetic meanings. For example, 'thought' (*sixiang*), when activated, becomes the dynamic verbal form 'thinking–perceiving' (*si–xiang*4), while 'existence (*cunzai*), when activated, becomes the higher level 'existing–being' (*cun–zai*5). In other words, Language Drift Theory is in essence a poetic methodology for philosophy, art and literature. Though it might be possible for rhetoric and objects to drift towards a certain essential category or value system, this category or system cannot escape a similar fate of drifting. It will be swept along by the language-

---

4 *Author's Note:* The hyphenated '*si–xiang* (思–想)' or '*cun-zai*' is considered a verbal form instead of a noun, revealing a state of drifting.

5 *Translator's Note:* This is a practice similar to that of Martin Heidegger, who hyphenated the German word *Dasein* as *Da-sein* and thus endowed the word with a new shade of meaning.

generating process, just as blockages on a mountainside get swept away by runoff from the mountaintop, or clouds in the sky get blown away by capricious winds. Therefore, the creativity of poetics does not originate from any ancient yet revived 'essence'; nor is it a mere imitation of any reality which is heavily burdened with a poetic pursuit. It is, instead, generated from reflections on the poetic artistry of languages and symbols in their drifting journey, with no set origin or definite destination. Language Drift Theory hopes to transcend such binary oppositions as subject versus object, form versus content, presentation versus representation, art versus reality, etc., which feature in the current theoretical framework of literary criticism.

The *Heart Sutra* is a perfect embodiment of Buddha's wisdom (thinking–perceiving) that is cautiously confined to a state prior to the generation of any concepts or knowledge. In this sutra, the Buddha first demonstrates some major approaches the human sensory system can use to interact with reality, such as the Five Skandhas, the Six Roots, the Six Kinds of Dust, the Four Noble Truths and the Twelve Links of Dependent Arising. He then shows how they all get dissolved in the emptiness of Prajnaparamita ('Perfection of Wisdom'), and are left adrift in pilgrimage until they achieve non-self (non-attachment) and spiritual awakening (enlightenment).

When the Buddha's 'thinking–perceiving' is considered in light of Language Drift Theory, various concepts of the Western intellectual tradition can be – with the best of intentions – sharply challenged. Conceptual categories, such as Plato's 'theory of Ideas', Aristotle's 'pure Form', Descartes's and Kant's 'rationalism', and Hegel's 'spirit', are all held up to the light, and found to be empty. This is not a deliberate dismissal of a particular civilisation, but instead represents a helpless thirsting to revive ancient Eastern civilisation on the eve of a Doomsday, when humans are to be destroyed by a world they themselves have created.

Numerous expositions and commentaries on the *Heart Sutra* have appeared over the generations, many of which have proven significant, both intellectually and in their insights. After a thorough enquiry into their purports, I here humbly, if only for the sake of self-soothing, venture to provide my own explanation of the text from the perspective of Language Drift Theory.

Lately, I have been constantly thinking about *Dandang*, an ordained Buddhist monk from a temple in the famous *Jizu* Mountain in western Yunnan Province, whom I deeply admire. Monk *Dandang* was named *Tang Tai* when he was born, and also went by his courtesy name (or *zi*), *Dalai*, or religious names, *Puhe* or *Tonghe*; but he was most commonly known by his self-chosen title (*hao*), *Dandang*.[6] As a master of poetry, calligraphy and painting of the early Qing period (1644–1911), *Dandang*'s painting and calligraphic works are believed to be of as much artistic value as that of the so-called Four

---

6 *Translator's Note:* Until the first decade of the twentieth century in China, a person usually had three names besides his or her surname: *ming*(名), *zi*(字) *and hao*(号). The *ming* is the name given by parents; *the zi* is the name granted to a person at the beginning of adulthood; and *the hao* is a less formal kind of name chosen by the person themselves. In the Confucian society of ancient China, people were commonly addressed by their *zi*. Many poets and writers in ancient China are known by their *hao* rather than their *ming* or *zi*.

Great Monk Painters (*Bada Shanren, Shi Tao, Hongren* and *Kun Can*), but have been overlooked by art history for over three hundred years. Only very recently has he been honoured together with these four monks and the term Five Great Monk Painters been recognised. I have therefore chosen some of his paintings as illustrations for the book, to show my appreciation, and to celebrate this long-deserved recognition.

In writing this book, I am deeply indebted to the following people for their insights into Buddha, Buddhism and the *Heart Sutra*: the American sinologist Bill Porter (also known as Red Pine); British writer Karen Armstrong; German writer Hermann Hesse; Chinese Buddhist master Hongyi; Chinese Buddhist master Mingyang; and Chinese scholars Lai Yonghai, Chen Qiuping and others. I have particularly benefitted from the Chinese version (translated by Ye Nan) of Red Pine's commentary, and Master Hongyi's commentary on the *Heart Sutra*. The incredible wisdom, guidance and insights of scholars throughout history and around the globe have been invaluable to me, like bells ringing along my path towards buddhahood.[7]

Li Sen
New Year's Day, 2017

---

7 Translator's Note: Here the author acknowledges the help of these scholars by comparing their insights to bells, which in Buddhist traditions symbolise wisdom and compassion. It is believed that the gentle ringing of bells serves to focus a practitioner's attention, drawing it away from future worries and past concerns, and to lead him or her closer to enlightenment.

Impossibility of Representation (#3). Shanshui painting with poem in running script calligraphy (album leaf), ink on paper, 20.3 × 24.2 cm, by Dan Dang.[8]

---

8 *Translator's Note:* Chinese *shanshui* painting (literally meaning 'mountain–water' painting) is generally considered one of the highest forms of expression in ancient Chinese art. Though often translated as 'landscape painting', it is actually unique, and very different to landscape painting in the Western tradition.

Chapter one

Chanting and Knocking

The *Heart Sutra* is a great work of art, of splendid rhetoric and unsurpassed beauty. It is a masterpiece that integrates all three dimensions of the philosophy of art (or poetics), namely, poetry, perception and expression. It is not to be read as a narrative, but to be chanted as verse. Chanting helps the mind find its unique rhythm, letting it unfold in its multiple manifestations. Ultimately, chanting is a way of discovering, creating or reviving the rhythm of mind. Discovering, in the sense that it salvages this lost or temporarily forgotten rhythm characterised by a yearning passion for spiritual liberty; creating, in the sense that it cultivates and nurtures this rhythm; and reviving, in the sense that it enables life to open up and flow freely. Chanting is the best manifestation of the poetic beauty in a piece of literary writing, since the yearning for chanting arises from the inborn spiritual pursuit for supreme good and supreme truth in the human heart. Though what is called 'supreme good' or 'supreme truth' might be nothing other than a slight touch of bubble-like good or a faint light of dream-like truth,[9] let us not stop chanting, for once chanting begins, salvation sets sail as wind arising from the river of mind and carries the meditator toward a state of prajna, dissolving the ego-self into emptiness.

---

9 *Translator's Note:* In Buddhism, bubbles and dreams are two commonly used metaphors for describing the illusory nature of existence. Other similar metaphors include a dewdrop, a phantom, a flash of lightning in a summer cloud, a flickering lamp, etc.

Let us chant *The Prajnaparamita Heart Sutra*:

 The noble Avalokiteshvara Bodhisattva,
 while practising the deep practice of Prajnaparamita,
 looked upon the Five Skandhas
 and seeing they were empty of self-existence,
5 said, 'Here, Shariputra,
 form is emptiness, emptiness is form;
 emptiness is not separate from form,
  form is not separate from emptiness;
 whatever is form is emptiness,
  whatever is emptiness is form.
 The same holds for sensation and perception,
  memory and consciousness.
10 Here, Shariputra, all dharmas are defined by emptiness,
 not birth or destruction, purity or defilement,
 completeness or deficiency.
 Therefore, in emptiness there is no form,
 no sensation, no perception, no memory and
  no consciousness;
 no eye, no ear, no nose, no tongue, no body and no mind;
15 no shape, no sound, no smell, no taste, no feeling and
  no thought;
 no element of perception, from eye to
  conceptual consciousness;
 no causal link, from ignorance to old age and death,
 and no end of causal link, from ignorance to old age
  and death;
 no suffering, no source, no relief, no path;
20 no knowledge, no attainment and no non-attainment;
  for nothing is to be attained.[10]

---

10 *Author's Note:* Previous versions of the *Heart Sutra* have traditionally punctuated before this line, but it seems more reasonable to me to punctuate after it, for the lines following this line display an obvious shift of calling to bodhisattvas, which forms a parallel with the earlier calling to Shariputra and later to 'all buddhas'. The sutra, as a whole, demonstrates a typical question-and-answer form of discourse.

>   Therefore, bodhisattvas, take refuge in Prajnaparamita
>   and live without walls of the mind.
>   Without walls of the mind and thus without fears,
> 25   you will see through delusions and finally nirvana.
>   All buddhas past, present and future
>   also take refuge in Prajnaparamita
>   and realise unexcelled, perfect enlightenment.
>   You should therefore know the great mantra of
>   Prajnaparamita,
> 30   the mantra of great magic,
>   the unexcelled mantra,
>   the mantra equal to the unequalled,
>   which heals all suffering and is true, not false,
>   the mantra in Prajnaparamita spoken thus:
> 35   'Gate gate, paragate, parasangate, bodhi svaha'.[11]

Chant, and chant continually. The rhetoric of the *Heart Sutra* is like a light of permanence shining on a dark road, or a swift boat that ferries us across the sea of suffering. Therefore, simply chant to be free of any worries about the meaning, and you will arrive at that state wherein you are one with the chant, with no distracting thoughts penetrating your consciousness, but only the sympathetic harmonics of your body, speech and mind together in one flowing gesture. The core of chanting lies not in the meaning behind the words, but in the light of permanence attained by the act of chanting, through the resonation of syllables with your

---

11 *Translator's Note:* The English translation is based on: Red Pine, *The Heart Sutra: The Womb of Buddhas*, Shoemaker & Hoard, 2004, p. 2. There is, however, a slight adaptation at lines 20–5 because the author made small changes there in the Chinese version (see Note 9). All quotations from translations by Red Pine, otherwise known as Bill Porter, in this book are from the same publication.

body. Chanting in itself is Buddhist faith manifested, or an ambience created, through which the person chanting fully experiences the ongoing of the spiritual pilgrimage. To chant is to set the self-nature on the path toward buddhahood, ferry it towards the bright world on the Other Shore, and attain enlightenment both of the person ferrying and for the person ferried. And the self-nature of chanting is intently perceived in the very chanting process, which naturally leads to the ecstasy of prajna (wisdom)[12].

Chant, and chant continually. Chanting kindles the ocean of sound whose rushing tidal waves pacify all suffering. Suffering is identical to the kalpas (aeons) of life; it is rooted in fear and results from ignorance of self-nature, which, through chanting, is brought back into light. Self-nature calls for a liberation of spirit and a transcendence beyond existence. It is, however, by no means equal to the self, in that self is drawn inwards, whereas self-nature opens up and unfolds in the wide open. It is thus certainly wrong to consider chanting a way to seek the self instead of self-nature. As the Indian sage Jiddu Krishnamurti puts it in *The Root of All Fear*:

> The craving to become causes fears; to be, to achieve, and so to depend engenders fear. The state of the non-fear is not negation, it is not the opposite of fear, nor is it courage. In understanding the cause

---

[12] *Translator's Note:* This sentence and the following paragraph allude to a teaching about self-nature by Huineng (638–713), also commonly known as the Sixth Patriarch of Chan, who is a semi-legendary but central figure in the early history of Chinese Chan Buddhism. Huineng taught that to perceive self-nature is to attain buddhahood and stressed the importance of 'seeing into one's own nature'.

of fear, there is its cessation, not the becoming courageous, for in all becoming there is the seed of fear. Dependence on things, on people, or on ideas breeds fear; dependence arises from ignorance, from the lack of self-knowledge, from inward poverty; fear causes uncertainty of mind-heart, preventing communication and understanding. Through self-awareness we begin to discover and so comprehend the cause of fear, not only the superficial but the deep casual and accumulative fears. Fear is both inborn and acquired; it is related to the past, and to free thought-feeling from it, the past must be comprehended through the present. The past is ever wanting to give birth to the present and so becomes the identifying memory of the 'me' and the 'mine', the 'I'. The self is the root of all fear.[13]

Continuous chanting brings about transmission of the Dharma and drifting of skandhas; the transmission of the Dharma is revealed through the oneness of the rhythm of word and life in their driftage. To set the *Heart Sutra* adrift is to explore and clarify the boundary of this transmission, rather than drawing life down to the depths of the abyss or luring it into a trap. Therefore, chanting is by nature a poetic practice devoid of depth structure, value judgement or historical burdens. The mind, deeply besieged by the material world and conceptual meanings, needs to take an urgent step to break down the

---

[13] *Translator's Note:* The English version is from: Jiddu Krishnamurti, *The Book of Life: Daily Meditations with Krishnamurti*, Harper One, 1995.

walls that trap it, set sail on its pilgrimage towards ultimate liberty of life, and attain self-redemption. From this perspective, chanting can be seen as a way to attain and to surpass the emptiness of the Dharma, for in the eyes of the Buddha, even physical appearances are emptiness; how more conceptual consciousness? As it is put in the *Diamond Sutra* (Section Five, 'Genuine Discernment of the Principle of Suchness'):

> 'Subhuti, what do you think, is it possible to see the Thus Come One [Tathagata] in his physical appearances?'
>
> 'No, World Honoured One, it is not possible to see the Thus Come One in his physical appearances. Why? Because the physical appearances mentioned by the Thus Come One has no physical appearance.' The Buddha said to Subhuti, 'All appearances are empty and false. If one sees all appearances as no appearances, then one sees the Thus Come One.'[14]

Chanting may take the powerful course of surging rivers, rushing in all directions, or the leisurely flight of geese migrating across the sky, or the forceful pattern of stirring wind blowing over the earth. Chanting offers self-protection and self-illumination by lighting up the past, present and future. In the process of chanting, I may be awakened at any line, and at any line where I am awakened, I experience self-liberation. The *Heart Sutra* is a very great poem that leads people from attachment towards understanding. Indeed, the

---

14 *Translator's Note:* The English version is from: Thich Nhat Hanh, *Chanting from the Heart,* Parallax Press, rev. ed., 2006.

chapter 'On Three Objections' in the *Mozi* elaborates on the consoling and healing power of music:

> In ancient times, when the lords were tired of governmental affairs, they found recreation in the music of bells and drums; when the ministers were tired of their office work, they found recreation in the music of pipes and strings; the farmers plowed the fields in spring, weeded them in summer, harvested in autumn, and stored the grains in winter. When tired, they also enjoyed themselves with the music of jars and vases.[15]

I chant the *Heart Sutra*, because it is a doorway of radiant emptiness opening into the soul. Yet this doorway has neither frame nor threshold. In my series of poems *House*, there is one called 'Knock'. It evokes the joy of liberating the self, of being one's own weathervane – the joy I feel as I chant the *Heart Sutra* in this mortal world plagued by vexation:

> **Remember**
> **At the foot of Mt Gong in Gaoli was a wooden house**
> **Outside the house was a wall, rocks crowding rocks**
> **Leaves crowding leaves**
> **There was a door panel, standing**
> **No hollow for shaft 'round which it might swing**
> **No chain by which it might lock**
> **Just standing**

---

[15] *Translator's Note*: The English version is from: *The Complete Works of Motzu in English*, translated by Cyrus Lee, The Commercial Press, 2009.

Remember
There was a child who tried to knock on that door
He said to those inside, please open the door
I need to tell you something
From inside came no response

Day after day he came to knock
The door never opened, only flowers opened their buds
He could only tell the crack between door and wall
What I needed to tell you is
'You are my love. I will tell you of my hate.'
This is the last thing he said as a child
The last time he knocked

(Translated by Nick Rosenbaum)

Winter Mountains (#9). *Shanshui* painting with poem in running script calligraphy (album leaf), ink on paper, 22.9 × 34.5 cm, by Dan Dang.

Chapter two

Call and Response

The *Heart Sutra* was written for everyone. It calls to everyone in the world, and everyone in the world calls out to it. Everyone in the world calls out to each other, their hearts adrift, floating on a pontoon bridge leading to the Other Shore. Each person is like an intoning word, or a group of words, placed at a threshold connecting such binary concepts as being and non-being, life and death, brightness and darkness, sense and non-sense. Both sides of the threshold call out. The *Heart Sutra* is like a moving threshold, crowded with numerous isolated items of rhetoric produced by the mind. These items of rhetoric are people, whose external being reveals their internal existence.

The *Heart Sutra* is a house of words, a place where rhetoric takes refuge for self-construction. It is the matrix of all pure language, within which infinite words originate, as the following little poem 'House', of mine reveals:

> That milky white – it's the swelling of the sky above. That unendurable, coagulated obscurity up there. And how will the peaches fare? Or the plums, or the crabapples? But mine is a suffering that collapses in an instant.
>
> I'm testing the season's new thunder, this thunder I've reared. All the saws are spitting out splinters, but where are the hands working them? This bellows I've made expels a quick blast of wind. There's a stooge gathering wood out on the hillside – off he goes with the trunk bobbing on his shoulder!

That's my house, with the thickly covered hill looming over it. There I have my turquoise roof; my books; my fire pit. Rain drips from the eaves – and so it does, wearing out the stones underneath, as it always has.

Outside my door bends a river, its flexure ever-present, rising up from the undisturbed river bed. The fish are not mine. They are a blade, sharpening themselves ceaselessly against the shimmering water. The boat is not mine. It is a hollowed-out hammer, emptied, drifting upon the river.

Sometimes I'm in my house, brewing tea beside the fire pit, practising letting go so that I can wait.

Now I'm outside, watching the fruit like roosted sparrows drawing toward my house. And out here I've seen nervous spring beams set summer ablaze, and mournful autumn clouds curl into clumps of winter snow.

The world is waiting for me to fling open the gates and peer out; the threshold waits for me to come back and cloister myself – this I know.

(Translated by Thomas Garbarini)

All great works of literature are chantable. But what is the point of chanting? My answer is – chanting is a form of calling.

All great calls are oriented towards 'emptiness', targeting those who are unreachable. Calls of this kind are thus even more compassionate, or full of pity. When the anonymous author of the *Heart Sutra*, a follower of Shakyamuni Buddha, put words to paper, his voice of calling roared through the universe with a divine might. The most compassionate call is of peace and joy, with its sound like soft ripples moving across the water's surface and passing throughout all ages into eternity.

Here the very act of writing is a call to *chuxin* ('beginner's mind'). The writer starts by calling upon an enlightened being, one who is continually shaped by different sorts of divine powers and driving forces – Avalokiteshvara Bodhisattva. With words like lightning bolts sparking across the sky, he conveys the first layer of meaning: 'The noble Avalokiteshvara Bodhisattva, while practising the deep practice of Prajnaparamita, looked upon the Five Skandhas and seeing they were empty of self-existence…' This calling brings Avalokiteshvara Bodhisattva fully into the spotlight as the compassionate central character of the *Heart Sutra*. In other words, this initial call is oriented towards the caller himself – a self-calling of the enlightened one.

Great works are by nature callings oriented towards the writers themselves. I may even venture to propose that the long-standing mystery about the identity of the author of the *Heart Sutra* is now solved – he is none other than the mysterious Avalokiteshvara Bodhisattva him/herself. This way of writing enables every chanter of the *Heart Sutra* to become the caller. Every calling entails a pleasant surprise, bred from a sudden insight into the world. Like the dawning of the first ray of sunshine, this feeling of surprise dwells in the heart of the chanter, causing him or her to feel he or she is Avalokiteshvara Bodhisattva in the flesh. In fact, Avalokiteshvara Bodhisattva is indeed capable of being manifested in whatever form is best suited for the situation. Avalokiteshvara alone among all the bodhisattvas was known for the ability to transform endlessly, drift continually, develop unceasingly, and appear as both male and female.

As American scholar Bill Porter[16] observes:

> I cannot help but conclude that Avalokiteshvara appears here as an incarnation of Maya, the Buddha's mother. Thus, Avalokiteshvara's name, meaning Lord of Those Who Look Down from On High, refers to her rebirth as the deva Santushita on the summit of Mount Sumeru, where she gained the perspective and the knowledge that enabled her to look down upon such conceptual systems as the Abhidharma. That she now appears as a male bodhisattva is in keeping with the early Buddhist notion that such rebirth was necessary for the cultivation and attainment of Buddhahood. However, Avalokiteshvara alone among bodhisattvas was also known for the ability to appear as a female, which was, no doubt, related to his previous incarnation as Maya. Another point worth noting is

---

16 *Translator's Note:* Bill Porter is an American author who translates under the pen-name Red Pine. He is a translator of Chinese, primarily Taoist and Buddhist texts, including poetry and sutras. In 2018 he won the American Academy of Arts & Letters Thornton Wilder Prize for translation.

that Avalokiteshvara is known to have thirty-three manifestations, the same number as the number of devas at the summit of Mount Sumeru.

(Bill Porter, p. 47)

In the eyes of ordinary people, Avalokiteshvara does indeed embody motherly compassion and the mercy of a goddess, upon whom they call in whatever circumstances.

The writer of the *Heart Sutra*, after calling upon Avalokiteshvara, proceeds to call upon Shariputra, the disciple of the Buddha, 'Here, Shariputra, form is emptiness, emptiness is form; emptiness is not separate from form, form is not separate from emptiness; whatever is form is emptiness, whatever is emptiness is form. The same holds for sensation and perception, memory and consciousness.' Prompted by the power created by continuous chanting in harmony with the rhythm of the mind, he then calls Shariputra a second time:

> Here, Shariputra, all dharmas are defined by emptiness, not birth or destruction, purity or defilement, completeness or deficiency. Therefore, in emptiness there is no form, no sensation, no perception, no memory and no consciousness; no eye, no ear, no nose, no tongue, no body and no mind; no shape, no sound, no smell, no taste, no feeling and no thought; no element of perception, from eye to conceptual consciousness; no causal link, from ignorance to old age and death, and no end of causal link, from ignorance to old age and death; no suffering, no source, no

relief, no path; no knowledge, no attainment and no non-attainment; for nothing is to be attained.

Next he calls upon the bodhisattvas, or you might say Avalokiteshvara or all enlightened beings put forward one more self-calling, 'Therefore, bodhisattvas take refuge in Prajnaparamita and live without walls of the mind. Without walls of the mind and thus without fears, they see through delusions and finally nirvana.' Having introduced the concept of 'emptiness' through repeated calling, the writer proceeds to call upon all buddhas – or again this can be viewed as another self-calling by Avalokiteshvara or all buddhas, 'All buddhas past, present and future also take refuge in Prajnaparamita and realise unexcelled, perfect enlightenment.' The sutra ends with a last call to the caller himself together with all those lost in this world, '*Gate gate, paragate, parasangate, bodhi svaha*', with the sound of calling merging with the flowing of the great mantra of Prajnaparamita into eternal time.

Calling guides the path towards the perfection of the Threefold Enlightenment (enlightenment of self, enlightenment of others, and perfection of enlightened practice), leading it into the boundless realm of the Dharma. While calling, the caller never lets go of language, which, though illusory and drifting, serves as a lifeline.

All calls aspire to be heard, whether by human beings or by things, for being heard is the essential meaning of their existence. While the Buddha declares that 'all dharmas are defined by emptiness' and everything eventually becomes nothing (emptiness in driftage), a call, whether by an enlightened one or an ordinary person, always embodies some sentiment and represents the soul's seeking for self-liberation with the accompaniment of sound and form. This is a significant point that must be made clear in referring to Buddhism. The Buddha surely taught avoidance of indulgence, but never advocated over-abstinence, for both indulgence and over-abstinence can be expressions of self-attachment that need to be treated as a psychological or physical illness. In fact, the Buddha himself led a life with human compassion. He returned, for example, together with his cousin, the monk Nanda, and his son Rahula, to Kapilavastu for a visit before his father King Suddhodana died. Though quiet after his father's death, his eyes were filled with tears. He sat in vigil beside the coffin and acted as one of the pall-bearers at the funeral procession. These actions exemplify the importance of love and empathy in Buddhist teachings.

Love or righteousness, as a skandha, are the manifestation of compassion, as are truth, kindness and beauty, which embody *chuxin* (beginner's mind). To love is to show compassion, and compassion calls upon compassion, like the mysterious expressions of poetry that call upon the poetic spirit. Calls of such kind can thus be considered as prajna manifested in love. A little poem of mine, 'Hear' tries to capture this idea.

O young Muse
   Again I hear you
Late that night
   A pass between mountains birthed a rooster
Your sewing machine
   Tugs at a blue spindle on the lake's surface
Your verdant meadow
   Ensnarls a thousand acres of cotton bolls
Your silkworm cocoon
   Shoots into a constellation suspended in empty sky
Your flowered poetry
   Hammers in a copper drum
Your objects
   Surge audibly into my homeland
In the barest of instants
   The walls that encircle me and my chimney
Clandestinely, grow warm

           (Translated by Nick Rosenbaum)

Calling requests a response. A call is in itself a response. As two mountain peaks call to each other, all peaks around the world stand in silence. As two rivers call to each other, all rivers around the world gush past rocks into the sea.

Calling is manifested through the vision of countless sails swelling out at sea, through the sound of military drums rattling across a vast battlefield, or through the spiritual progress along the Buddhist path towards liberation.

Sages. Hanging scroll, ink on paper, 108 x 59.3 cm, by Dan Dang.

Sages (detail),
by Dan Dang.

Chapter three

A Hero Poem

The *Heart Sutra* is a hero poem. The writer displays such superb concision in his ability to convey the perfect wisdom of the Buddha in such a brief space, and his mind is so broad and vision so lofty, that he can be nothing other than a true hero.

He starts by referencing not just the noble Avalokiteshvara, but also the perfect wisdom achieved by the Bodhisattva, who on looking upon the Five Skandhas saw 'they were empty of self-existence'. These simple first lines immediately introduce to the reader the five channels around which the mind is structured, namely, the Five Skandhas. The lines not only identify the Five Skandhas as the root cause of suffering, but further identify the path of practice as a means to overcome suffering. This straightforward style of writing presents itself in a mixture of extraordinary mightiness and absolute softness.

Hero poems are always in this style, because sages are generally succinct, unlike pathetic scribblers, who, as cowardly bookworms and shameful imitators, can merely quibble with pretentious writing or equivocate about empty concepts. But the way such poems combine internal mightiness with external sageliness, a feature known as 'mightiness within and sageliness without',[17] is often beyond the understanding of the ordinary mind. Communicating this extraordinary mightiness in such very plain language, the sutra is a perfect model of the Confucianist Doctrine of the Mean, with a beauty that is both firm and drifting.

---

17 *Translator's Note*: The original Chinese expression, *waisheng neiba* (外圣内霸), is reminiscent of the phrase 'sageliness within and kingliness without' (*neisheng waiwang*, 内圣外王), which first appeared in Zhuangzi's writings and was later proposed by Feng Youlan (in *A Short History of Chinese Philosophy*) as 'the leitmotif of Chinese philosophy'.

Avalokiteshvara Bodhisattva 'looked upon the Five Skandhas' and they were instantly found to be 'empty of self-existence'. What a straightforward declaration! What else is left to be said, given that all the Five Skandhas are empty of self-existence? Nothing but strength and mightiness.

Bill Porter observes:

> In the longer version of this sutra, the term *mahasattva* appears in apposition to *bodhisattva,* as it often does in Mahayana sutras. Literally, this means 'great being' or 'great hero', depending on how one understands *sattva.* Its earliest reference, however, was not to humans but to lions. Only later was it applied to those who shared the courage of the king of beasts. Although the term *bodhisattva* was used by other religious sects in ancient India before the advent of Buddhism, the compound *bodhisattva-mahasattva* was used exclusively by Buddhists.'
>
> (Red Pine, p. 43)

Great heroes write great poems of heroism. And this is especially the case for the *Heart Sutra*, which represents not only literary prajna, but more importantly prajna of action, that is action emphasising practice in which the mind and body are in harmony. Its Chinese version by Xuanzang (602–64) succeeds in presenting perfectly the heart, or most central insight, of Buddhism in no more than 260 Chinese characters. This is because the sutra is committed to dissolving rather than formulating concepts. It never goes to extremes; rather, it takes the middle way between 'making and breaking'. In such writing flows a poetic spirit that is simultaneously mighty and tranquil, a spirit that embodies a poetic pursuit of primitive simplicity, in which the world of objects and world of rhetoric come into existence with perfect purity.

The writing of a hero is in effect an act of self-redemption or self-realisation under the guidance of poetic spirit. In contrast, scribblers equivocate with empty statements and elaborate phrasing, only to create a torch for illuminating the concepts of others, rather than reflecting on themselves.

Victor Hugo said, 'Beyond absolutely correct revolution, there is absolutely correct humanism.' I would suggest, beyond absolutely correct value and meaning systems, there is also an absolutely correct realm void of any meaning.

Let us assume knowledge is classified into truth, goodness and beauty, with each existing on a different plane. Then the first of these should be the plane of truth, whose medium is scientific and instrumental rationality. This is the level of material existence, in which the natural and social sciences operate. The second is the plane of goodness, mediated by values and systems of meaning. This is the level of mental constructions, in which the humanities operate. The third is the plane of beauty, whose principle is 'art for art's sake', or to seek beauty divorced from any didactic, moral, or utilitarian function. This is the level of emptiness, where poetry and the spirits freely drift.

Present on all three planes is heroism, as well as accounts of heroic actions, but heroism in the highest sense is not set on discovering or creating scientific rationality, nor on creating or consolidating value systems, but rather on guiding those who are lost and freeing the lost from suffering and attachment.

In this sense, a hero poem is by no means one about reality or the mind, but one that focuses on emptiness. Siddhartha Gautama (the Buddha) was a great poet, as was the writer of the Heart Sutra. Such great poets are continually transforming mundane things into fresh literary symbols, thus producing numerous accounts of wisdom that drift in the realm of emptiness. These literary accounts are marked by both primitive simplicity and emptiness – primitive simplicity illuminates emptiness. The emptiness, at the same time, is manifestation of chuxin (beginner's mind) – emptiness *is* chuxin. Emptiness is different from non-being; it is instead the initial state of things, like a flower opening its pedals for the first time.

The Buddhist hero that has attained enlightenment for the self, as well as others, is not an all-seeing being, nor a holistic concept. This is an important point that must be made clear.

One outstanding feature of the conceiving–thinking of Buddhism is that it does not create a supreme being, making it markedly different from, for example, Christianity. Both the enlightenment of self in Hinayana and the enlightenment of others in Mahayana (which also involves an essential process of enlightenment of self) both instead focus on ferrying people to the Other Shore.

By not setting up a supreme being that transcends life, death and time, Buddhism leaves open the possibility of every person becoming a buddha, through achieving the fullness of the self-nature and being ferried to the Other Shore.

Of course the Buddha also goes by several other names. He is known to ordinary people, and in Hinayana, as Shakyamuni (Siddhartha Gautama), the founder of Buddhism. He is the

One Who Has Attained Full Enlightenment, and the One of Proper and Universal Knowledge. A bodhisattva, meanwhile, is a seeker of full enlightenment, or a buddha-to-be who has already generated bodhicitta ('enlightenment-mind'). Many Buddhist practitioners who have made it to the stage of bodhisattva eventually become a buddha. That explains why Avalokiteshvara Bodhisattva is at the level of looking upon the Five Skandhas and 'seeing they were empty of self-existence'.

Avalokiteshvara Bodhisattva (or the Goddess Guanyin) is an enlightened hero in the poetic sense, who is free of poetic pursuit or attachments. Like other heroes, Avalokiteshvara Bodhisattva is lonely, but this loneliness is a manifestation of the awakened self, rather than a result of the absence of bosom friends. This loneliness is with no cause or effect, and with no wind or waves.[18] It needs, however, to be manifested through the mobility of cause–effect and wind–waves so as to achieve the freedom of drifting in the poetic sense.

Heroism and love are two major themes of great works of literature. As I see it, a blending of these two is also a prominent recurring melody in such Buddhist sutras as the *Heart Sutra* and the *Diamond Sutra*.

The poem 'Returning Home', from my *Spring Shortage* poem series, is a case in point, which depicts how 'heroism' goes in search of 'love'.

> **A thousand horses, and not a single friendly voice;**
> **just hills, and sea; and hills, and sea.**

---

18 *Translator's Note*: The implication here is that the loneliness of Avalokiteshvara features perfect inner peace, like the tranquil sea with no wind or wave. It is being solitary, not desolation.

A thousand birds, and not a single friendly face;
just sky, and land; and sky, and land.
A thousand years, with nobody to call a friend;
just black, and white; and black, and white.
A thousand graves, and not a friend among them;
Just tall, and short; and tall, and short.
Oh, dear Muse! Our pact remains strong.
Two figures, since days long gone;
One ahead, one behind; one ahead, one behind.

(Translated by Thomas Garbarini)

People who seek bosom friends in this world must be heroes in some sense. Chinese cultural figures, like Boyi and his brother Shuqi, who chose to starve to death on Shouyangshan Mountain rather than eat grain from Zhou,[19] and the musician Yu Boya and his bosom friend the woodcutter Zhong Ziqi[20] are all heroes in the poetic sense. But the greatest hero of this kind is of course Siddhartha Gautama, the spiritual teacher of all ages.

---

19 *Translator's Note*: Boyi and Shuqi were brothers who lived in China at the time of the transition between the Shang Dynasty and the Zhou Dynasty. They are remembered in Chinese literary culture for their personal and moral virtue, loyalty and pacifistic idealism. In the 'Seven Admonishments' section of the *Chuci* anthology, the second piece, 'Drowning in the River', references Boyi and Shuqi with extravagant praise.

20 *Translator's Note*: Ziqi was an ordinary woodcutter who was nevertheless able to recognise what was in the heart of Boya as the latter played the qin (Chinese zither). When Boya was focusing on Mount Tai as he played, Ziqi said, 'Wonderful – as grand as Mount Tai!' When Boya's focus was flowing streams, Ziqi said, 'Vast and swelling, like flowing streams.' Whatever Boya described in his music, Ziqi intuited. When Ziqi died, Boya broke the strings of his qin and never played again. The Chinese idiom *gao shan liu shui* ('High mountains and flowing streams') is used to refer to such once-in-a-lifetime friendship.

Other heroes worthy of note include Socrates, the eternal tutor of youth, who faced death with absolute serenity; Li Dan (Laozi),[21] who rode off on the back of a water buffalo leaving society behind, and whose ideas resonated centuries later with Wittgenstein;[22] the poet–teacher Confucius, who used to teach and chant along the riverside with his disciples; Zhuang Zhou (Zhuangzi), who famously dreamt of being a butterfly, and told the story of a Peng bird, which, as a transformation of a Kun giant fish, flew from the northern darkness to the southern darkness;[23] Tao Yuanming, who, in a sudden spiritual awakening, rested his gaze upon the Southern mountain while plucking chrysanthemums by the eastern fence;[24] and of course, the Muses who give inspiration to writers, who in turn plant and grow rhetoric for literary creation like farmers planting crops on land.

---

21 *Translator's Note:* Li Dan (Laozi) was a Chinese philosopher and writer, believed to be a contemporary of Confucius during the 6th or 5th century BC. He is the reputed author of the *Dao De Jing*, founder of philosophical Daoism (Taoism), and a deity in religious Taoism and traditional Chinese religions.

22 *Translator's Note:* Wittgenstein is believed to have been heavily influenced by Taoism. For example, like Laozi, Wittgenstein also relied on language to try to communicate or show what cannot be encompassed by language.

23 *Translator's Note:* 'The Butterfly Dream' and the Peng bird story are both famous parables in the *Zhuangzi* (3rd century BC), one of two foundational texts of Daoism, along with the *Dao De Jing*. One day Zhuangzi fell asleep and dreamt he was a butterfly. When he woke up, he did not know whether he was a man who had dreamt he was a butterfly, or whether he was a butterfly now dreaming he was a man. A Peng bird is a giant bird that transforms from a giant fish called a Kun.

24 *Translator's Note:* Tao Qian (4th–5th centuries), also known as Tao Yuanming, was one of China's major poets and the greatest of his period. He spent much of his life as a recluse. This sentence indirectly quotes the fifth poem in his *Drinking Wine* series.

Lines by Tao Yuanming from his eighth poem in the *Imitating the Ancients* series best express how I feel: 'I do not see any intimate friends, except some old burial mounds. Along the road remain two tall graves, one for Boya and the other for Zhuang Zhou.'

The heart of a hero is the heart of prajna, and his love and compassion is the prajna in bloom. The hero poem is not written merely in words, but with one's whole being. When Huo Qubing,[25] the young hero of the Han Dynasty, led his troops on long campaigns and launched sudden attacks against invading enemies, their heroism resounded afar, transcending the boundaries of mind and lasting throughout the ages. The following poem of mine, 'The Stone Horse at Huo Qubing's Tomb', was written in memory of this heroism:

> Mount Qilian, Mount Qilian, Mount Qilian
> All flies submit to their wings,
> As all glittering wings submit to their flies;
> Only the General's stone horse submits to the wind
> Wasteland, wasteland, wasteland,
> Where my emptiness unfolds,
> The clopping hooves, his charger's cries,
> steep unto the sky
>
> (Translated by Thomas Garbarini)

---

25 *Translator's Note:* Huo Qubing (140–117 BC) was an outstanding and brave general of the Western Han period (206 BC–AD 24). He and his uncle, Wei Qing, led a campaign into the Gobi Desert of what is now Mongolia to defeat the Xiongnu nomadic confederation, winning decisive victories such as the Battle of Mobei in 119 BC, and bringing peace and prosperity to society.

Enjoying Peace and Prosperity. Hanging scroll, ink on paper, 116 x 55.6 cm, by Dan Dang.

Enjoying Peace and Prosperity (detail), by Dan Dang.

Chapter four

Dialogue and Enlightenment

From the very beginning, great works of literature have been anti-conceptual.

At the same time, great writers find it necessary to formulate concepts to enable expression of the grand ideas that swell in the human heart.

From the tension between the anti-conceptual and conceptual arises a passion, like the warm currents that supply nutrients to all beings. This is the poetic spirit bubbling and adrift in the human mind.

The poetic spirit searches for attentive listeners, people with whom a dialogue is possible. But not all people communicate in a poetic way. Most scholars, those obsessed with concepts in particular, can only communicate in a concept-oriented manner. How pathetic they are! Their minds are burdened with piles of lifeless concepts that blind them from seeing the truth.

There is a misconception among ordinary people that the use of concepts is necessary for communicating with sages, or that sages take pleasure in formulating concepts. Though this may be true of an ordinary intellectual, it is not true of the sages, whose communication through writing is by nature poetic, as is evident in the writings of Plato; of Li Dan (Laozi), the founder of Daoism (Taoism); and of the Confucian masters. When sages do create concepts, they do so for the sake of constructing a poetic path that leads to true knowledge and guides people from attachment towards understanding. The *Dao De Jing*[26] (or *Classic of the Way and Virtue*), as a long

---

[26] *Translator's Note:* Dao De Jing is a transliterated name of a Chinese classic text traditionally credited to the 6th-century BC sage Laozi

poem on the history of the mind, can be shuffled and randomised freely, with its poetic spirit unchanged and poetic power undiminished. Plato's *Republic*, a poetic drama on the history of the mind, is reputed for its rich literary devices: the metaphors of the cave, the line, the three beds and the sun, are all well-known in the history of philosophy (and also in the history of literature).

The history of mind as told by sages is a spiritual history of how rhetoric gets continually sharpened and regenerated in its drifting journey.

Conversing with the Buddha at the thinking–perceiving level, the author of the *Heart Sutra* stands visible to readers. But there are other invisible authors of the sutra – the Buddha; Avalokiteshvara Bodhisattva; Shariputra; and all buddhas past, present and future. The visible author converses with the invisible ones, making the *Heart Sutra* a completely open text. All great texts feature this kind of complete openness, perfect sincerity and unquestionable purity. Their words manifest *chuxin*, the open beginner's mind, from which they were generated and within which they go adrift.

The mind staying true to its open nature is not the mind of the physical being, the value system, or the Dharma.

It is instead skandhas of the mind awakened, self-realised and self-assured.

(also known as Lao Tzu or Lao-Tze). It is also published under other transliterations (Daodejing, Tao Te Ching, etc.), as well as *The Way and Its Power*, *Classic of the Way and Virtue*, etc. This book has chosen a similar way of transliterating other Chinese classics such as *Yi Jing* for *The Classic of Changes*, and *Shi Jing* for *The Classic of Poetry*.

It is not easily revealed. When one claims that one has a mind that is truly open, one does not really have it.

It does not sink down from the burden of language or objects, nor does it flutter about narcissistically.

It is the wisdom–mind blooming with prajna in the realm of emptiness–enlightenment.

The initial purpose of language is to facilitate communication. That explains why legendary texts written in old languages that have passed down from ancient times are presented in either dialogues or allegories. There is a similarity between the two, in that a dialogue is a conversation with human beings, while an allegory is a conversation with animals or objects. Both represent communications between human beings and the world.

All Buddhist scriptures are accounts of dialogic discourse. Where there is no dialogue, there is no writing.

Dialogue brings presence to the mind, which is in effect a field. From the perspective of Buddhist philosophy and of mine,[27] dialogue is not for the purpose of seeking 'essence', but for unfolding 'essential occurrence'. According to Martin Heidegger, dialogue helps the presence 'enter into the essential occurrence'. He says, 'Essence (*Wesen*) is merely represented, idea. Yet the essential occurrence (*Wesung*) is not merely the mere combination of the "what" and the "how" and thus a richer representation; instead, it is the

---

27 *Translator's Note:* The author refers to his Language Drift Theory, introduced in the Author's Preface and elaborated on in the following chapters.

more original unity of both.'[28] Essential occurrence seems to me to be another kind of skandha that achieves the presence of the unfolding of itself at the moment of going adrift. There is no unchanging or permanent essential occurrence, for it can 'become' instantly and disappear instantly through the dialogue.

The *Heart Sutra* exists in both a longer and a shorter version. The longer version, presented in a dialogic form, has the more typical format of a sutra. It provides context for the main teaching of the text with an introduction and conclusion, which some say were added by later generations. Part of the purpose of adding the context is to provide a scene with the Buddha's presence for a dialogue to happen and for the thinking–perceiving of the *Heart Sutra* to be recognised by the Buddha. Today's readers will find Avalokiteshvara Bodhisattva in this scene different from the common understanding of Avalokiteshvara Bodhisattva, whose identity stands adrift and undergoes constant changes while being shaped by different interpreters from different times and cultures. Below is the longer version of *The Prajnaparamita Heart Sutra,* which was translated into Chinese by Buddhist monks Prajna and Liyan.[29]

---

28 *Translator's Note:* English translation is from: Martin Heidegger, *Contributions to Philosophy (Of the Event),* translated by Richard Rojcewicz and Daniela Vallega-Neu, Indiana University Press, 2012, p. 227.

29 *Translator's Note:* Prajna (734–?) was an Indian monk who in 790 translated the longer version of the *Heart Sutra,* together with Liyan (710–95), a Buddhist monk from the Silk Road oasis of Kucha.

Thus, have I heard: Once when the Bhagavan was dwelling on Rajgir's Vulture Mountain together with a great assembly of bhikshus and a great assembly of bodhisattvas, he entered the samadhi known as Manifestation of the Deep. At that moment, the fearless Avalokiteshvara Bodhisattva was practising the deep practice of Prajnaparamita, and looking upon the Five Skandhas saw that they were empty of self-existence. By the power of the Buddha, the venerable Shariputra then asked the fearless Avalokiteshvara Bodhisattva, 'If any noble son or daughter were to practise the deep practice of Prajnaparamita, how should they be instructed?' Avalokiteshvara Bodhisattva answered, 'Shariputra, if any noble son or daughter were to practise the deep practice of Prajnaparamita, they should thus be instructed: "empty of self- existence are the Five Skandhas".'

'Here, Shariputra, form is emptiness, emptiness is form; emptiness is not separate from form, form is not separate from emptiness; whatever is form is emptiness, whatever is emptiness is form. The same holds for sensation and perception, memory and consciousness. Here, Shariputra, all dharmas are defined by emptiness, not birth or destruction, purity or defilement, completeness or deficiency.'

'Therefore, Shariputra, in emptiness there is no form, no sensation, no perception, no memory and no consciousness; no eye, no ear, no nose, no tongue, no body and no mind; no shape, no sound, no smell, no taste, no feeling and no thought; no element of perception, from eye to conceptual consciousness; no causal link, from ignorance to old age and death, and no end of causal link, from ignorance to old age and death; no suffering, no source, no relief, no path; no knowledge, no attainment and no non-attainment.'

'Therefore, Shariputra, without attainment, bodhisattvas take refuge in Prajnaparamita and live without walls of the mind. Without walls of the mind and thus without fears, they see through delusions and finally nirvana. All buddhas past, present, and future also take refuge in Prajnaparamita and realise unexcelled, perfect enlightenment.'

'You should therefore know the great mantra of Prajnaparamita, the mantra of great magic, the unexcelled mantra, the mantra equal to the unequalled, which heals all suffering and is true, not false, the mantra in Prajnaparamita spoken thus: *"Gate gate, para-gate, para-san-gate, bodhi svaha"*.'

'Thus, Shariputra, should fearless bodhisattvas be instructed to practise the deep practice of Prajnaparamita.'

At that moment, the Bhagavan rose from samadhi and praised Avalokiteshvara Bodhisattva, 'Well done, noble son, well done. So it is, noble son, so should the deep practice of Prajnaparamita be practised. As you have declared, so is it confirmed by all arhats and tathagatas.'

When the Bhagavan had finished speaking, the venerable Shariputra, the fearless Avalokiteshvara Bodhisattva, and all those present in the worlds of gods, humans, asuras, and gandharvas praised what the Bhagavan had proclaimed.

Thus concludes the Heart of Prajnaparamita.[30]

The main teaching component of the longer Chinese version is almost identical to the version by Xuanzang. But the dialogue between the various interlocutors present is expanded, with the scene shifting and words moving on; drifting one moment, gathering the next. This is similar to how the swaying of one tree is mirrored by the motion of the entire forest, or how the movement of one shadow cast by a form is imitated by all shadows.

In general, there exist three types of dialogue. The first type is dialogue between minds. It involves effective communication between two mind systems with the purpose of unfolding the skandhas of emotion, life and meaning, and achieving, in deep sincerity, mutual reflections on different 'essential occurrences'. The second type is dialogue that takes place on the rational or conceptual plane. It does not necessarily involve communication between specific minds, but is intended to bridge or tunnel a passageway between methodology and teleology, so as to break down the walls of existence and convey the mind across the abyss towards truth. The third type

---

30 *Translator's Note:* English translation from Red Pine, 2004, pp. 200-1.

is pseudo-dialogue, in which concepts, conceptual systems and logical systems remain isolated or engaged in self-talk, with no actual conversation going on. In short, these three types of dialogue refer, respectively, to the dialogue of life, which happens between life and art; the dialogue of being, which happens between philosophy and thought; and lack of dialogue, the so-called 'dialogue' that results from the stagnancy of language produced by the deadly academic machine.

Buddhist scriptures, including the *Heart Sutra* and the *Diamond Sutra*, present dialogue of the first type, or help guide to dialogue of the second type. Spiritual and poetic dialogues are all dialogues of skandhas, in which communication is only possible when skandhas freely drift and inter-transform. They bring about heart-to-heart harmony of all elements involved in the dialogue.

Once, when I was listening to the Cello Suites of Johann Sebastian Bach, the 'buddha of music',[31] outside my window thunder sounded in a clear sky, with changing clouds streaming past, and some words came to my mind, from which I later formed a little poem 'Thunders Splits the Sky':

> thunder splits the sky
> mushrooms sprout
> the sun warms
> ripening corn
>
> rain fills ditch
> vine hugs tree

---

31 *Translator's Note:* This is used as a term of admiration, implying that Bach's music and composition practice is similar to the state of buddhahood.

> grass grows green
> muntjacs comes out
> the valley is mute
> the mushrooms have no master
>
> (Translated by Thomas Garbarini)

In the dialogue with all things of the world, all things become the skandha in my mind; in the dialogue with people across the ages, people become the skandha in my mind. The purpose of dialogue is to transform humanity, mind, virtue and action into skandhas, which manifest the being of humans. One cannot converse directly with other people or objects without transforming them into skandhas. In the dialogue, there exist no abstract humans or objects, for no passageway is available on the level of abstraction. Jiddu Krishnamurti, the Indian sage and spiritual leader, wrote in the essay *Our Responsibility*: 'To transform the world, we must begin with ourselves; and what is important in beginning with ourselves is the intention. The intention must be to understand ourselves and not to leave it to others to transform themselves or to bring about a modified change through revolution, either of the left or of the right. It is important to understand that this is our responsibility, yours and mine; because, however small may be the world we live in, if we can transform ourselves, bring about a radically different point of view in our daily existence, then perhaps we shall affect the world at large, the extended relationship with others.'[32]

---

32 *Translator's Note:* The English version is from: Jiddu Krishnamurti, *The Book of Life – Daily Meditations with Krishnamurti*, HarperOne 1995.

Dialogue in essence is self-transformation and self-enlightenment with which the sun of prajna shines on one's heart.

In the sense of seeking Buddhist truth, enlightenment means the mind has attained a spiritual state of emptiness with a pure and decontaminated self-awareness. But in the sense of literary and artistic pursuit, the state of enlightenment means providing guidance as to what reality shows, while abandoning teaching with metaphor that hides behind reality.

The *Heart Sutra* blends dialogue and enlightenment in a perfect manner. The dialogue is presented with absolute straightforwardness, breaking apart concepts and conceptual metaphors used in the dialogue, through a process of 'making and breaking', so that skandhas can freely drift. Being part of the skandha of emptiness, 'non-existing' in the verbal form serves as an invisible, sharp tool for 'breaking'.

And this sharp tool of 'non-existing' actually works through the inter-dependence of the 'skandha of profound existence' and the 'skandha of profound non-existence'.

As the *Vimalakirti Nirdesa Sutra* records, once Vimalakirti said to the bodhisattvas present: 'Virtuous Ones, each of you please say something about the non-dual Dharma as you understand it.' And the bodhisattvas each provided his own understanding. For example, the bodhisattva 'Pure Interpretation' said: 'Activity (*you wei*) and non-activity (*wu wei*) are a duality, but if the mind is kept from all mental conditions it will be (void) like space and pure and clean wisdom will be free from all obstructions. This is initiation into the non-dual Dharma.' Manjusri Bodhisattva said: 'In my opinion, when all things are no longer within the province of either word or speech, and of either indication or knowledge, and are beyond questions and answers, this is initiation into the non-dual Dharma.' Then Manjusri asked Vimalakirti: 'All of us have spoken; please tell us what is the bodhisattva's initiation into the non-dual Dharma.' Vimalakirti 'kept silent without saying a word'.[33]

The relationship between dialogue and enlightenment is at times like that of drums and cymbals that compete with each other in taking the lead, and at times, like that of pears and peaches that stay where they are, 'forgetting each other on branches'.[34]

One day, when sitting on the threshold of a wooden cottage, I overheard the dialogue of four clay pots in their striving for self-redemption, and recorded their story in my poem 'Doorway'.

> Outside the deserted hut,
>   things squabble as they divide the emptiness;
>   rustmarks partition an iron hammer.
> There are four jugs by the doorway, unclaimed,
>   that haven't yet grown their tails.
> One is further away, catching rain,
>   readying its eyes for the great escape.

---

33 *Translator's Note:* The English version is: *The Vimalakirti Nirdesa Sutra*, translated and edited from the Chinese (Kumarajiva ed. T. 475) by Charles Luk (Lu K'uan Yi), 1972.

34 *Translator's Note:* This is a neologism based on 'forget each other in rivers and lakes', which comes from a parable told by Daoist sage Zhuangzi. 'When the springs dry up and the fish are left stranded on the ground, they spew each other with moisture and soak each with spit – but it would be much better if they could forget each other in rivers and lakes'.

Another is under the eaves, arching its curved belly,
posing as a speaker for the coming spring.
The third one, parched, is waiting for its soles to sprout
   so it can draw water from the well.
The fourth one clutches the doorframe,
   threatening to roam the earth
   and find the kiln from whence it came.
The hut stands bereft;
   damp dullness partitions a basket of chisels.

            (Translated by Thomas Garbarini)

An Idyllic Pastoral Scene (#11). Shanshui painting with poem in running script calligraphy (album leaf), ink on paper, 22.9 x 34.5 cm, by Dan Dang.

An Idyllic Pastoral Scene (#11) (detail), by Dan Dang.

Chapter five

The Beauty of Vyaavalokayati

The word *vyaavalokayati* presumes a subject who carries out the action of 'looking (down) upon', or a supreme being 'looking' from above.

As Bill Porter observed, *vyaavalokayati* means 'looking' in Sanskrit. In his words, 'the verb *avaloka* means "to look (down) upon", and *vya* is an emphatic. Hence, the literal meaning of *vya-avaloka-yati* is "to look down upon intently". Thus, Avalokiteshvara practises that which he was named; looking down from above, and, perhaps thereby betrays an association with the hill gods of ancient India, if not with the deva Santushita at the summit of Mount Sumeru.' (Bill Porter, p. 56). Bill Porter's implication is that Avalokiteshvara was the Buddha's mother who, after her death, reached the fourth of the six heavenly realms of Kamadhatu (the Realm of Desire) – the Tushita Heaven – and became a goddess. It is worth noting, however, that creating God is by no means the point of the Dharma. Instead, the Dharma stands alert against, and consistently rejects the notion of a self-existent supreme deity. This is a notion of utmost significance, which constitutes a decisive difference between Buddhist teachings (the Dharma) and Buddhism itself.

The Dharma is the law that is meant to sustain all beings of the world. It is oriented towards humanity, not the divine, and that is precisely what makes it great. It is based, not on a knowledge-driven reasoning or conceptual system, but on the human sensory and perceptual systems. Its greatness lies in the non-essential, non-ontological characteristics of its language framework, which is, in a sense, anti-language.

Therefore, what is looked down upon here is not an object, but the spiritual self, which is also what the Chinese translation, Guanzizai, literally suggests.[35] Seen from the perspective of drifting skandhas, it is to be understood as *guan–zi–zai*, or, 'looking–self–being', separated by rules. This 'looking down upon' is not a reflection of objects in the mind of the subject, but is an integration of both. It is therefore an unfolding of the self that might be interpreted as *guan–zi–xian*,[36] or 'looking–self–revelation'.

The revelation of things in the mind manifests the mind itself. That is to say, the time and space of the mind as revealed in *guan–shi–yin*[37], *guan–zi–zai*, and *guan–zi–xian* is the space and mind of skandhas, where skandhas are present or temporarily dwell. Here, skandhas and 'looking' are of the same structure – the skandhas are equivalent to looking and vice versa.

The revelation of prajna is accompanied by the revelation of skandhas and 'looking (down) upon'. The first lines, 'The noble Avalokiteshvara Bodhisattva, while practising the deep practice of Prajnaparamita…', depict how wisdom ferries the

---

35 *Translator's Note:* Guanzizai (观自在) was a rendering by Kumarajiva, and the one preferred by Xuanzang. It means 'looking down upon oneself'.

36 *Translator's Note:* Guan–zi–xian (观自现) is a neologism created by the author based on *guan–zi–zai*. Refer to Author's Preface, *Author's Note* 3 for the purpose of using rules to separate syllables.

37 *Translator's Note:* In some Sanskrit texts Avalokiteshvara Bodhisattva's name was also written Avalokitasvara. In such cases, it was translated into Chinese as Guanyin (观音), meaning 'He/She Who Looks Down Upon Cries', or as Guanshiyin (观世音), meaning 'He/She Who Looks Down Upon the Sounds (Cries) of the World', which was the rendering preferred by Kumarajiva.

practitioner across the water to the Other Shore, which is in effect the drifting of skandhas (that is, looking).

Ferrying (people across the water) implies the drifting of skandhas (looking).

In fact, there is no such place as 'the Other Shore' where one can physically arrive. It is only a metaphor.

The Other Shore is this shore. It is where you get on the raft and start on your journey.

As I see it, the act of 'looking (down) upon' viewed in a deeper sense is one generated neither from above nor from below, but from the original location. It is not an act of looking over there, towards someone else, from where I am, or someone else looking over here from where that person is; rather, it is an act of self-observation, self-reflection and self-enlightenment. It is an act of self-redemption.

Of course, from the ordinary Buddhist believer's perspective, 'looking down upon' is an act by the supreme being, who keeps an eye on the world, imparting love and compassion to all creation. This supreme being does not look at humans as equal, because he is depicted as infinitely higher than them.

The Dharma, on the other hand, does not presume a supreme being whose light shines upon the Earth, and views humans as aimless ants. Instead, it is oriented toward humans rather than gods. It even stands alert against the possibility of itself becoming an over-powerful subject that may bring harm to practitioners. In this sense, it is to be viewed not as an intellectual or conceptual system, but as the law of drifting between the Dharma and non-Dharma.

The difference between Buddhist teachings (the Dharma) and religious Buddhism is also revealed through their different understandings of 'looking (down) upon'.

'Looking (down) upon' in the sense of the Dharma implies that arrival has already happened, which may be understood as the arrival of light, sight or even poetic spirit. A poem of mine titled 'Arrival', from the *House* series, reads as follows:

> I've finally arrived at autumn,
>   and I've nothing to say.
> Presently, the pear trees have decided
>   to let all the pears fall.
> Next, they'll decide
>   to have the leaves fall too.
> I'm waiting
>   for a decision, for a response.
> The rumble of summer's falling curtain rolls
>   from south to north.
> But, ever so faintly, all I can make out are
>   the pear blossoms calling to the pears,
>   and the pears calling back.
>
>   (Translated by Thomas Garbarini)

Arrival implies, not the ending but the beginning of a skandha's revelation (temporary dwelling), like a tiny bud emerging on a lotus, or the rising wind before a coming storm. Though it may be easy to arrive at a 'distant place', it is extremely difficult to arrive at 'the self'. A 'distant place' lies in the realm of emptiness with no physical boundary, enabling one's spirit to travel freely; whereas the self lies in the realm of reality, which, being manifested in the domains of form and sound, may in itself be a spiritual obstruction, hard to crack open. To arrive at the self by the Dharma means to transform the 'unbearable heaviness of Being' on this shore into the 'lightness or emptiness of Being' on the Other Shore. And that is undoubtedly a challenging task.

'Looking (down) upon' is the samsara, or the cycle of reincarnation that takes place either from near to far, or vice versa; that is, both self-chained and self-liberated. Arrival can thus be achieved at any point of the spiritual and physical reincarnation. The arrival at enlightenment is the physical and spiritual being blooming. So the lines 'Looked upon the Five Skandhas and seeing they were empty of self-existence...' might be understood as 'the Five Skandhas looked upon me and my self-existence was seen as empty'.

'Looking (down) upon' is the spring sunshine quietly shining its beauty and achieving unconditional self-cultivation.

It is in essence a looking inward, a return of the heart to the beauty of harmony. Great figures throughout history have advocated the practices of *li xin* (ordaining conscience of the heart), *li yan* (passing on ideas in writing), *li fa* (formulating social regulations and laws), and *li de* (establishing moral principles for the people).[38] These were all initiated by the desire of individuals or groups to look inward and to return to an original, harmonious state of being.

---

38 *Translator's Note:* Of these four, *li de* (立德) and *li yan* (立言) originate from the 'Duke of Xiang' chapter of the *Zuozhuan*. Together with *li gong* (立功, to achieve great merits), they were acknowledged to be the Three Immortal Teachings (三不朽). *Li xin* (立心) was first proposed by Zhang Zai (1020–77), a Chinese philosopher of the Northern Song period.

Looking inward is returning to one's true self. As Huang Binghong stated in an essay titled *Lecture Notes on Traditional Chinese Painting Theory*,

> Human babies can laugh and cry before they can talk. They laugh when put under a bright light or the illuminating sun, but cry if put in a dark room. This shows they can distinguish black from white. The colours of black and white reflect the true essence of reality, while all other colours are no more than variants of the sunlight, and are thus mere illusions.[39]

Arriving at the beauty of harmony means to decontaminate the effects of illusions on people. It is, in Heidegger's terminology, the 'clearing of concealment', or, in Husserl's terminology, 'returning to things themselves'. The state of things in themselves is a state of being one with the beauty of harmony. It takes no external form and is devoid of contamination by the illusory world. It is reality as-it-is.

And this reality as-it-is is unmistakably visible when the beauty of harmony manifests itself: 'Therefore, Shariputra... bodhisattavas take refuge in Prajnaparamita and live without walls of the mind. Without walls of the mind and thus without fears, they see through delusions and finally nirvana.' As a famous poem by Wumen Huikai[40] puts it:

---

39 *Author's Note:* From Lu, Fusheng (ed.) *Art Essays by Huang Binhong*, Shanghai Literature And Art Press, 2012, p. 145.

40 *Translator's Note:* Wumen Huikai, was a Chinese Chan (禅) master of the Song period (960–1279). He is most famous for having compiled and commentated the 48-koan collection, *The Gateless Gate*, from which the quoted lines are taken. The English version of the poem is adapted from several anonymous translations available online.

Spring comes with its flowers, autumn with the moon,
   summer with breezes, winter with snow;
If useless things do not clutter your mind,
   every season is your best season.

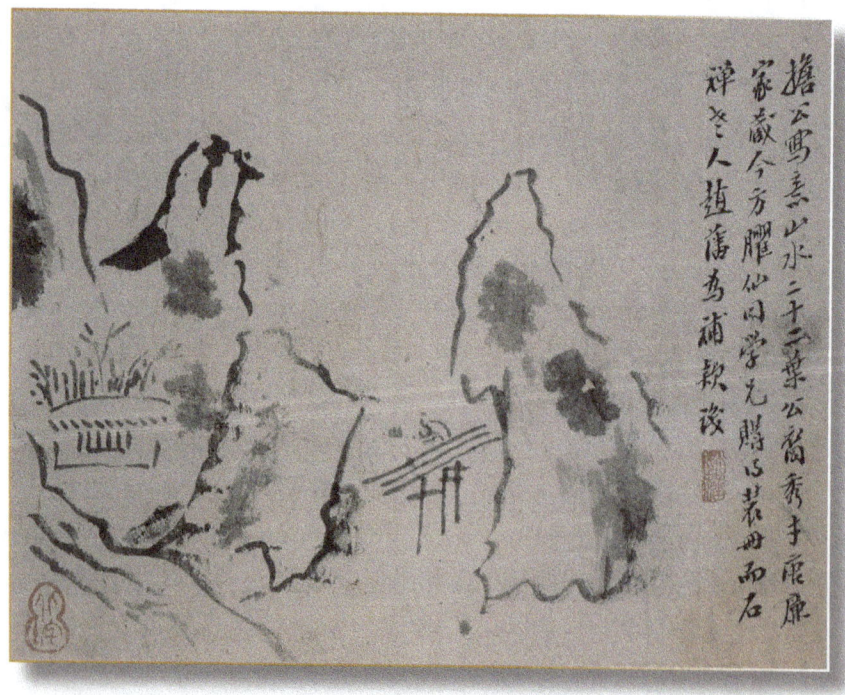

Enjoying Leisure Time (#2). Album leaf, ink on paper,
17.5 x 22.8 cm, by Dan Dang.

An Idyllic Pastoral Scene (#19). Shanshui painting with poem in running script calligraphy (album leaf), ink on paper, 27.8 x 37 cm, by Dan Dang.

Chapter six

The Language of Skandhas

The poem 'Cock-Crow', from my *Spring Light* series depicts a wave of sounds and forms (images), like the language of skandhas.

> The cock crows, drinking in the remnants of the sun.
> The cock coos, drinking in fleeting time.
> Its crows are chained together like the peaks of mountains,
> as swarms of incipient rainclouds hanging in the sky.
> Stones squeeze together beneath chafing branches.
> The mountain path undulates like breeze-blown silk.
> The cock crows empty, calling the world into spring.
> The cock crows panicked,
> calling mankind to cultivate their spirits.
> Soaring, the cock-crow brushes the sky with ink.
> Distant, the crock-crow meets ruddy despondency.
>
> (Translated by Thomas Garbarini)

In this wave of sounds and forms, I greet the skandha of cock-crow and drink together with it, talking in our native accent, in the same way that I embrace my melancholy in the season the peach trees blossom.

Yun, the Chinese for skandha, is defined in the *Shuowen Jiezi*[41] as 'accumulate', and in *Guangya*[42] as 'assemble'. Bill Porter observes, 'skandha has been alternatively translated into Chinese as *yin*, *zhong*, and can be understood as "to

---

[41] *Translator's Note:* The *Shuowen Jiezi* (说文解字) is a Han-period Chinese dictionary compiled in early 2nd century. Although not the first comprehensive Chinese character dictionary, it was the first to analyse the structure of characters and explain their etymology, as well as the first to use the principle of organisation by radical.

[42] *Translator's Note:* The *Guangya* (广雅), or 'Extended Erya', is a glossary dictionary compiled by the scholar Zhang Ji in the Three Kingdoms period (220–80). It was written as an extension of the more selective glossary the *Erya* (尔雅).

aggregate". The Buddha views the universe of our awareness as supported by Five Skandhas, namely, form, sensation, perception, memory and consciousness, which formed the basis for the subsequent development of the Abhidharma.'[43] The Abhidharma refers to the systematic Buddhist teachings.

The Dharma, whether manifest in the mind or in books, is a result of the aggregation of skandhas. As Bill Porter observes,

> The Sanskrit word skandha refers to the trunk of a tree, and I think the trunk of a banyan, or Ficus indica, might have been what the Buddha had in mind when he started using this term. The banyan is one of the world's most unusual trees. It begins as an aerial root that descends from a seed dropped by a bird in the canopy of another tree, such as a palm. After the seed sprouts, its root descends until it reaches the ground, and once established, it strangles its host. As it continues to grow, its branches put forth their own aerial roots, and these, in turn, form additional trunks. In the course of a hundred years, the original trunk becomes impossible to distinguish among the grove of roots that develop into trunks.
>
> (Bill Porter, p.57)

---

43 *Translator's Note:* The Chinese version of this quotation is ostensibly a translation of Bill Porter's explanation of 'Five Skandhas' in the 'Names, Terms, and Texts' list of his 2004 book. But the first sentence does not appear in the original English and seems to have been added by the Chinese translator. The second sentence in the original English is also slightly different from the Chinese version. So the English version provided here, though presented as a quotation, is mostly my own reverse translation.

Though it is not easy to verify Bill Porter's speculation about the relationship between the word 'skandha' and *Ficus Indica*, the analogy makes sense, for the way a single banyan root develops into a grove of trees, multiplying and occupying the space around, offers a precise metaphor for the way skandhas drift along as either dharmas or concepts.

The word 'skandha' is commonly viewed as a noun, a concept, but I believe it should be understood as a verb. 'Skandha' as a term needs to be defined, but the truth it signifies is ultimately unnamable. Assigning a name (noun) to something that cannot be named is the door to the Dharma of how language makes the impossible possible.

Skandha as a verb is the constant drifting and transforming of the Dharma, or the active self-manifesting of a vibrant mind. But 'the so-called buddhas and dharmas are not real buddhas and dharmas' (*Diamond Sutra*), for presenting the Dharma in text marks the end of it, rather than representing the real Dharma.

The Dharma drifts with help of language and ends with language.

The Dharma is language aggregated into skandhas, and skandhas are language-in-bloom.

The Dharma, in its vibrancy, joy and warmth, is a series of skandhas that are activated in the mind, over and over again, and drift across the land, reviving everything, like spring winds. Therefore, 'skandha' is not a concept with fixed connotation or denotation, but an illusion that drifts and keeps creating connotations. It is neither of emptiness nor of existence; it is an illusion that can be sensed and perceived.

Skandhas undergo an ever-changing transformation in the never-ending cycle of repeated birth, temporary existence, nirvana and rebirth. They can exist in an extremely small number, or in a great multitude. They can be the abyss of yin, or the energy of yang, or the intertwining and rotating of both, as presented in the Daoist (Taoist) yin–yang symbol[44] by Chen Tuan.[45] They are the meaning of existence, the poetic form of existence, and the heart as well as boundary of existence.

'Skandha' is the appearing of the non-appearing, the 'one' of all appearances, or all appearances of the 'one'.

In Xiong Shili's[46] words, 'There are two things that people cling to: the self and the universe. That explains why the Buddha presented a full analysis of these two and pointed out that they are none other than an aggregation of dharmas, like form and sensation. There is in fact neither real self nor real universe; instead, they are emptiness, like what is

---

44 *Translator's Note:* The yin-yang symbol is the most prominent Daoist symbol, also often called the *Taiji* symbol. It is composed of an outer circle enclosing two teardrop-shaped halves wrapped around each other. One half is black with a small white dot at its centre, and the other half is white with a small black dot at its centre.

45 *Translator's Note:* Chen Tuan (872–989) was a highly respected Daoist Master. It is said he revised the yin-yang symbol based on the Taiji image in the *Yi Jing* or *Book of Changes*.

46 *Translator's Note:* Xiong Shili (1885–1968) was the Chinese philosopher who has been widely credited as the thinker who laid down the basis for the revival of Confucianism in the twentieth century.

left when layer after layer of leaves are peeled away from a banana tree[47]: a hollow core.'[48]

Skandhas are like flocks of geese that migrate across the sky, leaving the sky with only emptiness and the mind with only a faint shadow. They are the flocks of geese being 'looked upon'; they are also the 'looking' by the geese themselves. They are the wailing of a single goose in wilderness; they are also the waggling of flocks of geese across the sky.

Skandhas can be compared to the unfurling of trees and their fruit. But from the perspective of human beings, trees and fruit are not aware of their unfurling. In my series of poems called *House*, there is one called 'The Pear Trees and the Pears' which reads:

> It is said that beyond the horizon, autumn deepens;
>   day breaks; and night winds in the valley bear pebbles.
> Robert Frost's ladder stretches into the pear tree,
>   higher than the leaves.
> Frost isn't there; only his saddle is.
> I'm not there; only my basket is.
> The pear is asking another pear —
>   all the pears are asking other pears.
> Why is the pear core sour —
>   sour since time immemorial?
> One pear says, this isn't up to the pear.
>   It's up to the pear tree.

---

47 *Translator's Note:* A banana or plantain tree is uniquely applicable to the Buddha's teaching about the emptiness of the Five Skandhas, because the stalk of a banana or plantain tree is made up of overlapping leaves surrounding a hollow core.

48 *Author's Note:* Xiong Shili, *A Glossary of Buddhist Terms*, Shanghai Bookstore Press, 2007, p. 21.

The pear tree suddenly shudders. A tree says,
  perhaps it's up to the white flower of the spring.
Another tree says,
  perhaps it's the verdant wind, the wet rain,
the march of time.
And another tree says,
  is it not that long ladder? And those wooden stools?
The sun arcs across the sky and the pears quiet.
  The sun dips beyond the mountains,
hiding the yellow of the pears.

               (Translated by Thomas Garbarini)

This is an allegory poem. Both the trees and the fruit are skandhas that produce further skandhas, and poetic spirit is generated at the same time. The skandhas that are produced from the mother-skandhas of the 'pear trees' and the 'pears' are also engaged in reproduction of pear trees and pears. Through the process, skandhas keep emerging and being submerged; and the subjective 'I' emerges and is submerged with them.

Skandhas drift, and so do people. Language gives birth to skandhas, and skandhas also give birth to language. Language is skandhas, and skandhas are languages. From skandhas the world is generated, and from the world skandhas are also generated.

That being said, I suddenly came to the awareness that skandhas, though explicable, do not have a fixed meaning. Or perhaps it is exactly this flexibility in approaching their meaning that makes the mind merry and joyful. To further elaborate this point, I quote several classical poems by

Buddhist masters of ancient times[49].

One
Inert or alert, all is Buddha;
but action does not follow understanding.
Muddled, chasing the material;
obscured, unable to find the way back.

Two
When I heard the gospel of Buddha,
undying and immortal,
I understood all beings are Buddha,
and I cursed my squandered time.

Three
Reflecting on the eternal reality of Buddha,
rejecting the world of illusion.
Now that I have seen the essence of all dharmas,
there is no real or unreal.

Four
Though I have escaped the four mortal vexations,
I have not broken free from the six Eternal Bases.
Illusions still cloud my vision,
which seem as airborne flowers.

Five
Upon my sudden enlightenment,
I understood that Buddha nature courses through everything.
Yet still, like an undepleted stream,
my awakening was incomplete, and the moon remained hazy.

(Poems translated by Thomas Barbarini)

---

49 *Author's Note:* The five poems are quoted from: Master Ming Yang, *The Essentials of Buddhism*, Shanghai Ancient Books Publishing House. 2007, pp. 322-323.

O skandhas, you who are manifest in the language of thousands and thousands of poems; you who have penetrated minds throughout the ages – come and rescue me.

O skandhas, you who are the raft to ferry me across the water; you who are the light to liberate my soul – come and rescue me.

Enjoying Leisure Time (#3). Album leaf, Ink on paper, 17.5 x 22.8 cm, by Dan Dang.

Chapter seven

Emptiness is Wind

The Buddha spoke the folllowing *gatha* ('verse')[50] as recorded in the *Diamond Sutra*, Chapter 26, 'The Dharma Body has No Marks':

> **If one sees me in forms,**
> **If one seeks me in sounds,**
> **He practises a deviant way,**
> **And cannot see the Tathagata.**[51]

Emptiness, or *shunyata* in Sanskrit, refers to the illusory essence of the mind, or the delusion seen through by the one who has attained awareness. It is defined by the nature of illusion, which is devoid of inherent existence.

Emptiness is the standing point from which the Buddha practises the Dharma.

The Dharma, or teachings of the Buddha, when viewed as a philosophy, is to be distinguished from Buddhism as a religion. It is in a sense an anti-philosophy[52] if examined from the perspective of traditional Western philosophies.

Buddhist philosophy is characterised by its non-duality – which is precisely where its greatness shines – being both

---

50 *Translator's Note: Gatha* in Sanskrit means 'song' or 'verse'. In Buddhism, it refers to special sayings of the Buddha or other Buddhist masters in prose or verse.

51 *Translator's Note:* The English translation is from: Hsüan Hua, *The Diamond Sutra: A General Explanation of the Vajra Prajna Paramita Sutra*, Buddhist Text Translation Society, 1974. Subsequent quotations from the *Diamond Sutra* are also from this translation.

52 *Translator's note:* Jacques Lacan first coined the term 'anti-philosophy'. Buddhist philosophy is an anti-philosophy in that it is not a systematisation of knowledge built on the use of a discursive mode of reasoning anchored in the certainty or transparency of ego-consciousness, according to an Aristotelian either–or logic.

self-constructing and self-denying, both forward striving and backward stepping, both boundary setting and boundary dissolving. Dancing between these various modes of being, it is the 'philosophy as an activity',[53] or the philosophical activity of a non-philosophy.

An anti-philosophy teaches against concepts, dogma and doctrinaire skandhas.

And Language Drift Theory focuses on casting adrift the skandhas that have been assembled in mind.

In the eyes of an activity-oriented philosophy (or a philosophy of verbs), concepts are dead. But just as Buddhist philosophy resorts to concepts in elaborating the idea of skandhas, so, too, an anti-philosophy finds concepts indispensable. Or put another way, just as concepts are indispensable for Buddhist philosophy in elaborating on the idea of skandhas, so are they indispensable for an anti-philosophy.

A skandha going adrift and unfolding itself brings about the presence of one or infinitely many concepts; and skandha as a concept represents the temporary existence of a 'drifting' moment – either the moment of finishing off or the moment of starting off.

As I have said, 'skandha' in the Language Drift Theory is to be understood as a verb. So are all other concepts.

---

53 *Translator's note:* Wittgenstein famously claimed, 'Philosophy is not a theory but an activity', thereby emphasising the difference between his philosophy and traditional philosophy.

Alain Badiou points out in his *Manifesto for Philosophy*, '[T]he conceptual operators by which philosophy configurates its conditions generally place thinking about time under the paradigm of one or several of these conditions. A generic procedure, close to its original eventful site, or confronted by the impasses of its persistence, serves as the main referent for the deployment of the compossibility of the conditions.'[54] Or to put it in a Buddhist way, the 'generic procedure' of language sweeps numerous skandhas along, driving them forward, walking, running or flying.

For Buddhist philosophy, emptiness is an indispensable conceptual site – a site in this context can be the noun form of a verb in temporary existence, or a sudden impetus of languages.

And like all other Buddhist concepts, emptiness is a skandha; it acts as a non-eventful site for a linguistic event.

In the framework of Buddhist philosophy, which is to be viewed as a philosophy of verbs, all concepts are to be perceived or used as verbs.

A philosophy of verbs has no subject or object; the predicate verb is all that is needed. In other words, a sentence or proposition is comprised solely of a predicate chain; all words in this chain, including concepts, exist in a drifting state.

---

54 *Translator's Note:* The English translation is from: Badiou, A., *Manifesto for Philosophy*, State University of New York Press, Albany, 1999, p. 41. Subsequent quotations from *Manifesto for Philosophy* are also from this translation.

This predicate verb or chain marks the path for the mind to float. And from this perspective, not only the concept of emptiness, but also the noble Avalokiteshvara Bodhisattva, Shariputra, and all buddhas past, present and future, become paths for predicate verbs to drift along.

The first line of the Sutra '[T]he noble Avalokiteshvara Bodhisattva, while practising the deep practice of Prajnaparamita' is precisely a demonstration of skandhas drifting on such a path.

Emptiness, however, is more than one path – it is to be seen as infinitely many paths as well as infinitely many skandhas. For example, when emptiness is further elucidated in the sutra, readers might recognise the viewpoint or voice of the Buddha himself: 'Here, Shariputra, form is emptiness, emptiness is form....' Of course, one may also identify the voice with that of Avalokiteshvara Bodhisattva, or other bodhisattvas, or that of Shariputra, or other disciples, or all buddhas past, present and future.

The emptiness-skandha sweeps together with it a myriad of voices, images, forms, rhythms or meanings.

Every attempt by emptiness to explore new paths is an effort to establish fresh boundaries as well as breaking through old ones. For instance, with the pronouncement 'all the Five Skandhas are empty of self-existence', emptiness conveys its conceptual meaning, and is breathed into the connotative existence of the Five Skandhas, which in turn further clarifies emptiness.

It should be noted that emptiness is possible to be defined clearly enough only when it is perceived as a drifting skandha.

The question is, is emptiness something bigger than skandha and Dharma? Some reasoning frameworks[55] might view emptiness as a spacious container capable of accommodating a multitude of skandhas. But emptiness as a superordinate concept of skandhas is actually a misconception.

The truth is, emptiness drifts about close to the various conceptual meanings of skandha, and the two can be considered interchangeable concepts. In other words, emptiness is isomorphic with skandha in terms of connotation and denotation, hence, 'form is emptiness, emptiness is form', for emptiness and form as isomorphic skandhas are like two sides of the same coin. Likewise, other skandhas are isomorphic with emptiness.

Skandhas float about within emptiness; emptiness drifts along, acting and counteracting with all other skandhas.

Emptiness is illusory; matter, all matter, is real. Illusion and reality are interdependent; they mutually beget each other. Both, however, are but provisional names. They and their endless mutual reproduction exemplify the drifting activity of skandhas.

Emptiness is a skandha; it is simultaneously mother of skandhas, or a driving force for the reproduction of skandhas. This so-called driving force, which is also self-driven and self-revealing, gets neutralised by the birth of new skandhas.

---

55 *Author's note:* These refer to, for instance, reasoning frameworks based on dualistic concepts like 'being' and 'non-being', 'illusion' and 'reality', or 'empty' and 'non-empty'.

Thus, emptiness offers an opportunity as well as an impetus for language to create the mental world. This opportunity or impetus drives appearances to ceaselessly generate new ones, until the eventual birth of categories of the mind system and the language system.

Along with the aggregation and dispersion of skandhas, appearances change and reveal themselves, displaying a lack of permanent self-essence.

Changes of appearance in themselves are not to be viewed as real or unreal, for the process involves nothing but the mind and words; but the mind and words are sources of dharmas, whose changes involve that of the names of temporary appearances.

'Dharma' in this context can be understood as Idea (in a Platonic sense), which provides a governing pattern for the world. Both, however, are only concepts created by the mind rather than the law behind the existence of appearances. For instance, a flower may be conceived as 'red' by man, but not so by a dog, for dogs are unable to perceive colour. So 'red' is a created concept. This ability to perceive colour is a randomly obtained capability, or perhaps, a transcendental ability endowed to humans by 'God'.

We are in fact talking about something real by means of a name which is in unreal existence. Or we may also elaborate on something that does not really exist with the use of a provisional name – 'God' is an example in point.

In the case of red roses, none of the 'red' colour, or the metaphor of the colour, or any conceptions about the expression ('red roses'), has ever really existed, for the 'red rose' metaphor was absent in the ancient Chinese conceptual system. But over time, the way things are perceived and exist in people's cognition has changed.

Dharmas are empty.

Appearances are neither empty nor real.

In the framework of Language Drift Theory, appearance is understood as the transformation, aggregation and dispersion of appearances. This is a revolutionary[56] perspective on the interpretation of Buddhist sutras.

The ten thousand dharmas assemble and disperse, and the Dharma takes its shape; the ten thousand appearances assemble and disperse, and appearance shows its form.

For the sustenance of the mind, we are bound to hold on to appearances and skandhas. Unfortunately, in so doing, the mind ends up trapped in attachments[57].

Eventually, civilisations, cultures and customs always turn into some type of attachment, notion or means of represen-

---

56 *Translator's note:* Appearance as a Buddhist term used to be interpreted within the conceptual system and has been invariably considered a noun. Language Drift Theory instead stresses the drifting state of appearances and creatively views appearance as a predicate verb, or conceptual site (in Alain Badiou's words). This clearly distinguishes Language Drift Theory from previous modes of interpretation.

57 *Translator's note:* In Buddhism attachment is considered the reason people are trapped in the endless cycle of birth and death. Freeing oneself from attachment is a crucial part of the journey in Buddhism.

tation. These in turn form patterns or chunks in the representational system, which are then conveniently paved in the mind, and eventually constitute structures of the mind.

The mind is a field where skandhas arise, exist and transform themselves.

Only when the mind field is non-empty is the existence of inbuilt culture or notion possible. But the fact is, there is no evidence of such an existence, since cultures or notions are ultimately only habits, beliefs, or certain expression systems with words acquired through observation and learning. They have, however, come to shape our view of the world. This, of course, is far from being an individual worldview; rather, it refers to a society's shared worldview based on shared culture or notions. When we try to make sense of the world through this worldview, we end up in a multitude of mental hindrances of attachment, which consequently bring forth heaps of illusory perceptions of reality.

Any cultural system of concepts, however grandiose the wording it adopts, or attractive or joyful it appears, represents merely dancing in fetters – that is, hindrances of attachment in the mind – rather than the true existence of individuals.

Existence of entities in the mind is a flower bred from dependent occurrences.

Attachment to existence is a gratuitous wound of the mind.

Emptiness would heal this dharma-wound of the mind, as the poem 'The Lotus and the Ploughshare' from my *House* poetry series depicts:

> Lotus upon Gold Sands River; ploughshare upon Jade Dragon Peak;
> Their master is the glimmer in the cave.
> They've never met; they just stay there, looking toward one another longingly.
> Year after year, their love passes from flower to flower,
> Rambling from Tiger Leaping Gorge to Spruce Meadow.
> Snaking through the rattans, coming out from the forest, writing Dongba glyphs.
> The waters of Lijiang. The moon above Kunming.
> The light in a study.
> Illuminates a wooden stool, a cup of tea, a bowl of ash.
>
> (Translated by Thomas Garbarini)

The lotus flower and the ploughshare, though unlikely to meet in reality, do meet in the imaginary world created by language. Here, the lotus flower, the ploughshare and language are all empty; emptiness serves as the force that drives skandhas, that is, appearances, into driftage. At this moment emptiness becomes isomorphic with the poetic spirit, and the poetic spirit, in going adrift, activates the emptiness of the ten thousand skandhas/appearances.

Emptiness is the path for skandhas; skandha is the evidence of emptiness.

Skandha is a flying bird; it is also graffiti of the bird.[58]

---

58 *Translator's note:* Graffiti of the bird is no longer the real bird.

With the drifting about of skandhas, the ten thousand appearances transform into flying birds.[59]

The graffitied bird knows not the real bird.

But in emptiness, the two birds join each other to become one. This is a decision made instantly at the moment when the mind, object and language meet through dialogue; it reflects the faith that the mind holds on to amid delusions.

A truly liberated person is defined by emptiness, or can be seen as a skandha completely freed from any attachment. Like the seed of a skandha, he springs up from the wet earth and savours his beauty in emptiness.

Emptiness is wind. Wind traverses the land; and I traverse the land in the wind.

I am memory of the past, or the flame of past memories consumed before nirvana.

Emptiness is the heart. My heart is saddened, when the ten thousand appearances gratuitously assemble and disperse.

Emptiness is the wind. I am saddened, when the wind arises from an empty cave and brings a mixed feeling of bitter-sweetness.

---

59 *Translator's note:* In Buddhism, birds are used to teach ethics and concepts. They are metaphors for our muddled, unskilful selves, and also represent our best, no-self selves.

Enjoying Leisure Time (#4). Album leaf, ink on paper, 17.5 x 22.8 cm, by Dan Dang.

Chapter eight

The Prayer Wheel of Language

In my *Shangrila* poem series, there is a poem called 'Prayer Wheel':

> Turn, brass, resonant chimes
> Upright axel, the only crux of your revolution
> Chant, original sin of the flesh, avaricious mule
> For the suffering concealed on your tongue, create language
> Chant, doubt of the blooming flower,
> the redemption of outcome
> For the ploughshare and the harrow tines,
> earthward traction
>
> (Translated by Thomas Garbarini)

The prayer wheel keeps turning; it is a skandha, a language and a heart; it is the wheel itself. It is emptiness, or the harmony of emptiness and reality; it is 'I', the subject. It is the aggregation of the Dharma; it is also the annihilation of the Dharma.

The prayer wheel turns between existence and non-existence, between true emptiness and marvellous (or wonderful) existence.[60]

The turning is ultimately initiated by the skandha of language, which chants itself into the infinity of emptiness.

Language drifts; it elaborates the beauty of words. Its chantable rhythm chain exists not simply for revealing meaning or idea, but, more importantly, for freedom of expression. Being in itself a kind of enlightenment, freedom serves as the path to prajna.

---

60 *Translator's note*: 'True emptiness' and 'marvellous existence' are Buddhist terms, referring respectively to the emptiness of non-emptiness and the existence of non-existence.

Meaning is not of interest for artistic expressions. What matters instead is the linguistic 'site' being distinctly manifested as if in bright light, free yet powerfully. This 'bright' manifestation or 'visual' revelation is similar in effect to an orchid's extraordinary appearance with its startling beauty and fragrance.[61]

Only ordinary writers take meaning revelation as the ultimate goal for written expression. In other words, ordinary writers, and their readers search for meaning, for meaning and revelation must be the ultimate goal. Some however, exploit language by ignoring the mysterious profundity of the drift activity of the language-skandha.

Ordinary people tend to equate the presence of meaning with the presence of truth or knowledge. In reality, however, truth in a metaphysical or poetic system is but a phantom; it is a 'generic procedure' for expression, which implies the temporary existence, that is, aggregation, of skandhas at various linguistic 'sites'.

Alain Badiou claims in his *Manifesto for Philosophy*:

> The specific role of philosophy is to propose a unified conceptual space in which naming takes place of events that serve as the point of departure for truth procedures. Philosophy seeks to gather together all the additional-names. It deals within thought with

---

[61] *Translator's note:* Orchids are regarded as noble and pure in Chinese culture, as they often flower in such inaccessible places as high mountains and deep valleys.

> the compossible nature of the procedures that condition it. It does not establish any truth but it sets a locus of truths. It configurates the generic procedures through a welcoming, a sheltering, built up with reference to their disparate simultaneity. Philosophy sets out to think its time by putting the state of procedures conditioning it into a common place. Its operations, whatever they may be, always aim to think 'together', to configurate within an unique exercise of thought the epochal disposition of the matheme, poem, political invention and love (or the event status of the Two). In this sense, philosophy's sole question is indeed that of the truth. Not that it produces any, but because it offers a mode of access to the unity of a moment of truths, a conceptual site in which the generic procedures are thought of as compossible. (p.33)

The assembling or dispersing of language reflects free expression; it confirms as well as decodes, through expression, the 'sites' of expressional procedures.

A so-called 'site' is where temporary existence occurs. It marks the chantable rhythm of life; it signals the realisation of semantic representation.

The drifting of rhythm is the drifting of skandhas. It is the spirit of life surging and rushing amid the wild waves of language, carrying along sometimes the beginnings of language, sometimes the illusory self, which is in constant state of flux.

Skandhas are created and go into driftage with no set goals; no one knows where a skandha starts, or what will eventually become of it. Skandhas remain in a free state of existence, reminiscent of how the Chinese poet Su Shi famously summarised the secrets of literary writing:

> Not liable to set rules, a good piece of writing moves on freely and smoothly like floating clouds or flowing water. Clouds drift and form new skyscapes every other day; a good writer develops most fitting styles for different purposes. Water shapes its course according to the nature of the ground over which it flows; a good writer works out his excellence in relation to the material about which he is writing. Thus is created the natural unity and coherence of writing with rich spontaneous creativity.'[62]

The *Heart Sutra* begins by 'gathering together all the additional-names' and setting the 'locus of truths' (Badiou): 'The noble Avalokiteshvara Bodhisattva, while practising the deep practice of Prajnaparamita, looked upon the Five Skandhas and seeing they were empty of self-existence...'. The presence of various types of skandha creates a 'site' in which concepts and state of procedures are 'compossible'. In the meantime, the drifting procedure of skandhas is initiated — as time and space first come into being, so does meaning

---

62 *Translator's note:* Su Shi (1037–1101), courtesy name (*zi*) Zizhan, literary name (*hao*) Dongpo Jushi, also called Su Dongpo, was one of China's greatest poets and essayists, as well as an accomplished calligrapher and public official. The quote here is from 'In Reply to Xie Minshi', a letter to a much younger writer who was a faithful follower.

first become manifest, and truth unfolds its first bud; it is the moment when *rupa*-skandha just starts to be represented in forms and appearances.

So the author goes on to explain *rupa*-skandha. If revelation of meaning, or idea, is the purpose, the line 'form is emptiness' says it all. Since both form and emptiness are now used as predicate verbs, they are sure to reveal the self in the drifting procedure, otherwise the movement would turn awkward, like someone singing out of rhythm. This revealing of self, similar to the flowing of breath in singing, is initiated by a passion in life and retained by flowing with the rhythms of life.

That is why 'form is emptiness' must be complemented by 'emptiness is form', even though the former phrase has made clear what is meant. In both phrases, the skandha that comes first is stressed and the one that follows left unstressed. When the stress pattern is reversed and balance is achieved, chanting, now in harmony with the breath, turns enjoyable and gratifying. It then vanishes along with emptiness and form, just as dust is shaken off loneliness by drum beats.

It is not over yet. The flow of the rhythm, or the driftage of skandhas, continues with the line 'emptiness is not separate from form, form is not separate from emptiness', before it comes to a temporary rest. It rests, as if relieved for now after the strong pronouncement of a firm belief, or after successful release from a bondage of loneliness.

The call of the sutra might be strong, but the phrasing is moderate. In discussing the Five Skandhas, which have been claimed to be 'empty of self-existence', the author remains firm by concentrating on the skandha of form. He presents an equation between form and emptiness, extends the same equation to the other four skandhas, and then concludes with subtly beautiful but impressively moderate words: 'The same holds for sensation and perception, memory and consciousness.'

In a similarly moderate manner, the sutra goes on. 'Therefore in emptiness there is no form, no sensation, no perception, no memory and no consciousness; no eye, no ear, no nose, no tongue, no body and no mind; no shape, no sound, no smell, no taste, no feeling and no thought; no element of perception, from eye to conceptual consciousness; no causal link, from ignorance to old age and death, and no end of causal link, from ignorance to old age and death.'

These are words of life being proclaimed and to be passed on through ages; they are skandhas setting out to driftage, or language being renewed, for endless regeneration; they are evidence of the overflowing beauty of an epochal masterpiece in human civilisation.

The prayer wheel of language keeps turning; with it the naming of reality through language turns empty.

The prayer wheel of language keeps turning; every 'site' of the turning serves as the start as well as end point for the driftage of skandhas.

And with its turning, all attachments are disposed of; all delusions are put to an end.

But how very hard it is to be detached from the skandhas of life! This I compare to the sound of black swans in a poem called 'Grey Swan' from my *Spring Water* poem series. I, Li Sen, am the grey swan, and my heart is the thunder in the poem.

> The grey swan in the sky,
>   calls to a cart beneath the mountain, Spring hears
> The grey swan in the wilderness,
>   calls to a wooden bridge over the river, Spring hears
> Grey swan calls grey swan,
>   two swans caged in two sheets of rain
> Thunder calls thunder,
>   two thunders in destiny's sequence,
> smashing against the same cliff

(Translated by Thomas Garbarini)

Enjoying Leisure Time (#9). Album leaf, ink on paper, 17.5 x 22.8 cm, by Dan Dang.

Chapter nine

All Dharmas are Empty

The caller calls; the calling reaches the caller. Through calling, a sentient being removes the veil of illusion and acquires a new vision, just like a piece of iron obtaining its transformed life as a shining sword. Through calling, the deluded heart breaks free from bondage and crosses over to the Other Shore, just as I, transformed into a ploughshare, stand unfettered by spring water.

The poem 'a plough' from my *Spring Water* poetry series reads,

> on the spring riverbank,
> a plough is chewing cud,
> a ray of light is wearing down stones
> a plough stupefies
> the oxen tilling the fields,
> a ray of light inches by carrying potatoes
> on the spring riverbank,
> a shoulder pole is meandering,
> a pair of baskets are sleepwalking
> charnel spring,
> the rooster stands in mournful silence,
> rusting into a pile of scarlet iron
>
> (Translated by Thomas Garbarini)

All dharmas are empty; all appearances are illusory. Both are like transient flowers at the spring shore, in full bloom today but following the flow of air tomorrow.

So the author of the *Heart Sutra* called, 'Here, Shariputra, all dharmas are defined by emptiness.' It is a calling from both human beings and buddhas.

'Buddha' in this context can refer to any of the buddhas: the Buddha of the past, Buddha of the present, Buddha of the future,[63] or buddhas of any other kinds. It can also refer to the Buddha nature[64] in every heart, or Buddhist teachings that are accessible to every being.

I quietly call to the Buddha, 'Revered One of the World, all appearances are empty; all dharmas are empty; all poetic feelings are empty.'

Over and over again I call to the Buddha, 'Revered One of the World, all dharmas are empty appearances; all appearances are empty dharmas; like transient flowers, they are but delusions.'

Buddhas are appearances, skandhas and dharmas; they are emptiness in a state of drifting.

The Dharma is illusory like flowers, whose days are as fleeting as a shadow. All dharmas are also illusory like flowers; they exist as but a passing shadow.

But the buddha in my heart is not a Buddhist buddha, but the one of poetry.

In fact, the reasoning framework of Buddhist teachings leaves no room for the existence of buddhas, for, in claiming that all dharmas are empty, Buddhist philosophy declares that all skandhas, including buddhas, are empty. The pronouncement exemplifies the great Buddhist thinking—perceiving that

---

63 *Translator's note:* The buddhas of the past, present and future are collectively called the Buddhas of the Three Times.

64 *Translator's note:* Buddha nature is believed to be the fundamental nature of all beings. Part of this fundamental nature is the tenet that all beings may realise enlightenment.

is devoid of attachments, completely empty, and bred only in the purest of minds. It sheds light on every single corner of the mind, leaving not an inch in the dark.

With the poetic spirit sent adrift, 'emptiness' the noun turns into 'being empty' the predicate.

'Being empty' is not nothingness; instead, it is what transforms in the mind, through drifting, into 'marvellous existence' — the existence of non-existence.

Following 'all dharmas are defined by emptiness', the sutra goes on to explain what the statement means. For this purpose, the author sets about expounding on what characterises a dharma by endowing emptiness (which is also a skandha) with connotations: 'Not birth or destruction, purity or defilement, completeness or deficiency'. This meaning endowment offers a path towards assembling skandhas and thus reveals their drift trajectory. For in this context, any elaboration otherwise is doomed to fail.

Where language fails to reach, only drifting skandhas functioning as predicate verbs prove effective. Therefore, 'all dharmas are defined by emptiness' can be understood as drifting skandhas 'being empty' and generating a myriad of skandhas.

Qu Yuan, the great poet[65], similarly resorts to external things (defined by emptiness) for the expression of mel-

---

65 *Translator's note:* Qu Yuan (339–278 BC) was one of the greatest poets of ancient China, whose highly original and imaginative verse had an enormous influence over early Chinese poetry. He was also famous as an upright statesman, who drowned himself in the Miluo River as a protest against the corrupt times. This event is commemorated annually in the Dragon Boat Festival.

ancholy and wistfulness, in an attempt to convey the lovesickness of the Lady and Lord of the River Xiang,

> The Child of God, descending the northern bank,
> Turns on me her eyes that are dark with longing.
> Gently the wind of autumn whispers;
> On the waves of the Dong-ting lake the leaves are falling.
>
> Over the white sedge I gaze out wildly;
> For a tryst is made to meet my love this evening.
> But why should the birds gather in the duckweed?
> And what are the nets doing in the tree-tops?
>
> The Yuan has its angelicas, the Li has its orchids:
> And I think of my lady, but dare not tell it,
> As with trembling heart I gaze on the distance
> Over the swiftly moving waters.[66]
>
> (Translated by David Hawkes)

Human feelings and external things follow on from each other, just as skandhas and the mind attend each other.

The feeling of melancholy, so beautifully depicted in the poem, is of a Buddhist nature – through resorting to external things, the melancholy mind is healed and the suffering spirit is liberated.

Emptiness is not only a doctrine for Buddhism; it also signifies the awakening or liberation of the mind. The concept

---

66 *Translator's note:* The Chinese poem titled 'The Lady of the Xiang' is from Qu Yuan's *Jiu Ge* (Nine Songs) poetry series. The English translation is from *The Songs of the South: An Ancient Chinese Anthology of Poems by Qu Yuan and Other Poets*, translated and introduced by David Hawkes, Penguin Group, USA, 2011.

originates from Nagarjuna's[67] famous statement, 'dependent arising is emptiness',[68] and has been considered the point of departure for Buddhist philosophical argumentation.

'Dependent arising' interrelates and interacts with 'emptiness'. To quote Professor Lai Yonghai of Nanjing University on this topic:

> Emptiness is the core concept of the Prajnaparamita sutras of Mahayana. It holds that all things are conditioned by multiple interdependent causes (hence, dependent arising) and are in a state of constant change. When conditions are appropriate, they arise, or, 'become'; when conditions become difficult, they pass away, or, cease to be. All things are in a perpetual process of arising and passing away, ever 'becoming' and never actually 'being'. They are devoid of any sort of independent or intrinsic nature, and are, therefore, 'empty'.
>
>> As cornerstone texts of the Prajnaparamita group of sutras, the *Diamond Sutra* and *Heart Sutra* are also grounded in the teaching that 'dependent arising is emptiness', but they both work hard to further elaborate on emptiness by focusing on the concepts

---

67 *Translator's note*: Nagarjuna (150–250), sometimes referred to as the 'second Buddha' in Tibetan and East Asian Mahayana traditions, was an Indian Buddhist monk and philosopher. He systematised Mahayana Buddhist philosophy around the central concept of the emptiness (*shunyata*) of all existents (dharmas).

68 *Translator's Note:* 'Dependent arising' is another way to express 'dependent origination', a core teaching of the Buddha, which points to how all things come into being reliant on other causes and conditions.

of 'breaking' and 'detaching'. In respect of 'breaking', the *Diamond Sutra* presents such well-known lines as: 'All conditioned dharmas are like dreams, illusions, bubbles, or shadows; like drops of dew, or flashes of lightning. Contemplate them thus.' This illustrates to the fullest a seeking to break the delusions of appearances. As for 'detaching', another famous line in the *Diamond Sutra* reads: '[fearless bodhisattvas] should give birth to a mind that is not attached to anything'. This reflects the striving to free the mind from attachments. The *Heart Sutra*, likewise, presents widely acknowledged form–emptiness statements, a crystal-clear elaboration on how to break the delusions caused by the Five Skandhas: 'form is emptiness, emptiness is form; emptiness is not separate from form, form is not separate from emptiness; whatever is form is emptiness, whatever is emptiness is form. The same holds for sensation and perception, memory and consciousness.' And the line 'live without walls of the mind' clarifies how to get detached. In short, both sutras explain emptiness from the perspectives of breaking external delusions and achieving internal detachment.[69]

On the other hand, 'dependent arising' and 'emptiness' are both dharmas in the state of drifting. Hence, 'all dharmas are defined by emptiness'. But it is immediately followed by the negation of a group of qualities: 'not birth or destruction, purity or defilement, completeness or deficiency' – does the

---

69 *Author's Note:* Lai, Yonghai, *Thirteen Buddhist Sutras*, Zhonghua Book Company (original book in Chinese), 2010, 'Preface' p. 3.

negation imply the presence of any dharma with permanent existence? Is there, after all, an existence of some sort of common appearance, or 'uniting element in the variety', something similar to Plato's 'Idea', or Plotinus' 'the One',[70] which stays untainted or unaffected, beyond the myriad particular appearances (or, specific skandhas)? In brief, is emptiness likely to possess an intrinsic nature? This is a difficult question for both Buddhist philosophy and the *Heart Sutra*. Below the statement 'all dharmas are empty' lies something profound and unfathomable, like an abyss, beyond the reach of language (a semantic black hole), about which, according to Wittgenstein, 'one must be silent'.[71]

Faced with this semantic black hole where language fails but upon which essentialists have insisted expounding, the *Heart Sutra* seeks to fill the gap with a series of negation. It first acknowledges the existence of skandhas, then negates it, along with dharmas and 'dependent arising'. In so doing, it dispels them all as provisional names.

During this process, 'being empty', as the predicate verb sent adrift, flies across emptiness like a graceful flock of geese in the sky, leaving behind emptiness, and at the same time negating emptiness.

---

70 *Translator's note:* Plotinus (205–70) was a major philosopher in Roman Egypt, who is known as the greatest of the Neo-Platonists. In his philosophy, described in the *Enneads*, there are three principles: the One, the Intellect, and the Soul. The One created the universe by progressive emanation, first into a purely spiritual form, Intellect, then into Soul, which in turn animated the physical world.

71 *Translator's note:* This refers to the statement 'whereof one cannot speak, thereof one must be silent' by Ludwig Wittgenstein, who is alluding to the language barrier in trying to describe consciousness.

Nevertheless, emptiness is also a skandha serving as a specific locus of drifting for the mind, and a kind of logic behind the existence of phenomena-appearances. Therefore, conceptualisation (assembling) and de-conceptualisation (dispelling) of emptiness are both inevitable outcomes of circumstances.

That is to say, the presumed so-called 'common appearance' or 'uniting element' turns out to be an unsurmountable wall, or a bottomless abyss. The drifting act of emptiness as explained in the *Heart Sutra* is a letting-go of the common appearance, specific appearances and the myriad dependent arisings that shape the mind. This is absolute detachment as illustrated in the following lines: 'Therefore, Shariputra, in emptiness there is no form, no sensation, no perception, no memory and no consciousness; no eye, no ear, no nose, no tongue, no body and no mind; no shape, no sound, no smell, no taste, no feeling and no thought; no element of perception, from eye to conceptual consciousness; no causal link, from ignorance to old age and death, and no end of causal link, from ignorance to old age and death; no suffering, no source, no relief, no path; no knowledge, no attainment and no non-attainment; for nothing is to be attained.' What is negated here includes the existence of the Five Skandhas, the Six Roots (Powers of Sensation), the Six Kinds of Dust (Domains of Sensation), the Eighteen Elements of Perception, and the Four Noble Truths. All are defined as being non-existent. Nothing can be grasped, therefore all are illusory; and such is the true reality.

But instead of providing a pessimistic philosophical view, the thinking–perceiving as shown in 'all dharmas are empty' represents, as I see it, a joyful non-essentialistic outlook. It is an anti-philosophy of the highest level.

An anti-philosophy is fundamentally anti-logic and anti-language. It calls for an act of drifting through poetic creativity to attain happiness and peace.

It should be noted, however, that poetic quality in the ordinary sense is in itself an attachment. It needs to be created and recreated through the drift of language. Essentially, poetic quality is not born poetic; it results only from 'once-again' being born or a re-affirmation of skandhas in the mind. Readers may refer to the following poem of mine, '*orange in field*'.

> sunrise in the southeast
> orange in field
> yellow amid orange
> yang amid orange
> yin amid orange
> orange beside orange
> orange within house
>
> sundown in the west
> orange in field
> twilight amid orange
> gloom covers orange
> moon on eave
> night without orange

(Translated by Thomas Garbarini)

Truly great poetic quality, in its attainment gets dissolved into emptiness and ends up in self-negation. Emptiness and self-negation are two paths leading to enlightenment.

In announcing 'all dharmas are empty', the *Heart Sutra* offers a rebuttal against doctrines of the Sarvastivada, an early school of Buddhism that arose around three hundred years after the Buddha's nirvana. The Sarvastivadins held to the existence of dharmas in all of the Three Times, namely, the past, present and future. Their doctrines, as I see it, were characterised by essentialism and represented the academicism in Buddhist philosophy. In assuming that dharmas are existent, they actually affirmed the capability of language to capture the real existence of matters or ideas.

But the Sarvastivadin beliefs did not conform to Buddhist teachings; the 'permanent existence of dharmas' they advocated was by no means identical to the 'marvellous existence' (existence of non-existence) taught by the Buddha.

As great Buddhist classics, the *Heart Sutra* and the *Diamond Sutra* transcend the constraints of academicism. Primarily they rebut the Sarvastivadin concept that dharmas are ultimate, discrete entities, maintaining that dharmas are also delusions to be broken or attachments to be abandoned. It should be noted that the 'breaking' in this context does not bring about any 'building', but results in emptiness, as is stated in the *Diamond Sutra*, 'All conditioned dharmas are like dreams, illusions, bubbles, or shadows; like drops of dew, or flashes of lightning. Contemplate them thus.' Of course, the 'emptiness' of dharmas does not imply a void; instead, it refers to the impermanence of dharmas. Like skandhas, dharmas remain adrift; they have to be assembled for conceptualisation, but at the same time they have to be broken as delusions.

Marvellous existence (existence of non-existence) occurs somewhere between the breaking versus building. It takes its form in the continually arising skandhas of poetry; it takes shape in the mutual begetting of emptiness and existence.

Marvellous existence (existence of non-existence) is skandhas adrift and skandhas in momentary existence.

I said, 'All dharmas are empty; emptiness occurs between arising and passing away, like the fleeting shadows of flowers.'

I then said, 'All appearances are empty dharmas; like flowers and shadows they co-exist with each other, and mutually reflect each other.'

Enjoying Leisure Time (#14). Album leaf, ink on paper, 17.5 x 22.8 cm, by Dan Dang.

Chapter ten

Thus have I Said

Let me begin this chapter by chanting 'The Exquisite Zither', a poem by Li Shangyin[72] of the late Tang period.

> I wonder why this splendid zither has fifty strings
>   Every string, every peg evokes those glorious springs
> Perplexed as the sage, waking from his butterfly dream
>   Like the king, entrust to the cuckoo my heart evergreen
> The moon bathes the teardrop pearl in the blue sea
>   The sun lights the radiant jade in indigo mountain
> These feelings remain a cherished memory
>   But I was already lost at that moment
>
>   (Translated by Lien W. S. and Foo C. W.)

Thus have I said: the *Heart Sutra* is like a piece of zither music with incomparable beauty and power.

Throughout history, people with extraordinary talents have found it impossible not to use language or 'speaking'. To speak is human; human beings exist in language, or, 'speaking'. Speaking thrives in the infinity of language.

Resorting to language is, in essence, a painstaking striving to do the impossible.

Speaking may turn out to be a practice of the prajna mind; it may also end up as self-imprisonment.

The idealist way of practising Prajnaparamita is to transform, through speaking, the painstaking striving of the mind

---

[72] Li Shangyin (813–58), courtesy name (*zi*) Yishan, is a Chinese poet remembered for the elegance and obscurity of his poems. 'The Exquisite Zither' is Li Shangyin's most famous poem, and yet it is also one of the most mysterious poems of the Chinese poetic tradition.

into joy. And this is what makes Buddhism, as an anti-philosophy, distinct from other contemporary anti-philosophies in the West.

Joy is, in the first place, mercy to the self.

The Dharma is a dharma of joy based on shared feelings and mutual affinity.

In other words, speaking, ideally, is an attempt by the mind to achieve communication and understanding – however wide apart they are from each other. This is the case with the speaking and chanting of the *Heart Sutra*.

The subtle part of the Dharma, as an anti-philosophy, lies in its capability to liberate the mind. Delivering the mind from myriad burdens, it replaces burdens with joy, hence: 'bodhisattavas take refuge in Prajnaparamita, and live without walls of the mind. Without walls of the mind and thus without fears, they see through delusions and finally nirvana.' The Dharma of prajna creates communication channels for the mind, and, in the meantime, abandons these channels that are adrift as skandhas. That is to say, though language is used as a makeshift remedy, it is nevertheless regarded as completely pointless.

The Dharma-derived joy is the top-level joy to be experienced at a spiritual 'site'; it is joy in the purest sense, devoid of defilement from any type of value system.

This joy experiences joy in the drifting of language or 'speaking'. But joy in itself is empty; like transient flowers, it is defined by emptiness.

Language, or speaking, is capable of going adrift; this fact proves its emptiness. When we speak about an orchid, we do not have to see the orchid with our eyes; when we speak of a stone, we do not have to hold the stone.

Emptiness is a basket woven with language, facts and the mind all combined.

Note that the basket is a metaphor and a skandha; it 'becomes' a basket, without having to be a real one. It is emptiness filled with joy.

Skandhas, as drifting emptiness, are bound to bear certain connotations, the realness of which is nonetheless nowhere to be affirmed. This, in fact, is also a kind of 'fear'. But the pursuit of realness serves as a driving force for skandhas, in seeking connotations, to go adrift. This driving force, as a nourishing force of life, is indispensable to human beings in retaining vitality.

Take love as an example. Love is a driving force of life; and proving the real existence of love has been one major inspiration of life, without which, humans are bound to be caught by a kind of 'fear of existence'. Therefore, the necessity to speak and the futility of speaking form a paradox that cannot be escaped by the skandha of life, nor by language.

Life, in terms of its awareness or experience of 'being', is a skandha. It aimlessly drifts and revolves in the world.

Being a skandha of emptiness, life is most earnest in seeking for something real or truthful. This earnestness stems from fear.

The author of the *Heart Sutra* is also confronted with fear: the fear of inability to grasp the truth of existence. Thus he tries to convince himself by repeatedly affirming the power of Prajnaparamita: 'You should therefore know the great mantra of Prajnaparamita, the mantra of great magic, the unexcelled mantra, the mantra equal to the unequalled, which heals all suffering and is true, not false.' This is more a 'faith' in, than an affirmation of, truthfulness. With conviction, fear of emptiness turns into joy of emptiness.

In fact, life that has achieved awakening ultimately brings nothing more than a joy of emptiness. Likewise, thinking–perceiving, as awakened thought, is nothing more than joyful thoughts on emptiness.

The joy is joy in emptiness and of emptiness; it is empty of emptiness. Joy of this kind can be said to be joy of the real sense.

The poetic quality of joy lies in the drifting of language.

The 'necessity to speak', in the *Heart Sutra*, places the activities of language somewhere in between metaphysical and physical systems – or, a 'mid-physical' position between 'breaking' and 'building'. The production of a good piece of writing and the generation of skandhas (such as thinking–perceiving) are similar examples. To break is to deconstruct; to build is to construct; to go beyond break or build by staying in between is to go beyond emptiness (or the Way, or Idea) and reality.

Joy is talent freely springing forth.

Only at a problematic moment of needing to speak but not finding the words is a marvellous existence (existence of non-existence) likely to occur.

Speaking makes no sense at the self-awakening moment of the spirit, but it is the only way to ease the pressure of silence (in Wittgenstein's terms). Of course, silence could be another way of 'speaking', but in such cases, it is to be distinguished from silence not functioning as a mode of expression.

'What is above forms is the Way; what is below forms are concrete things.'[73] The Way is a common, shared appearance, while 'concrete things' are specific appearances. Speaking is capable of assuming the existence of a common appearance that is 'not birth or destruction, purity or defilement, completeness or deficiency', or focusing on specific appearances, which can be real appearances or objects.

What language can do with the common appearance is only to 'assume' or 'hypothesise'; but with specific appearances, it 'describes'. This is a choice made by language itself.

To 'assume' implies an absence of root or substance with the origin. As the departure point of speaking, it provides insights into the relationship between language and the world.

---

[73] *Translator's Note:* The Chinese quotation is from the *Xi ci* commentary on the *Yi Jing*, or *Book of Changes*. The distinction between 'what is above forms' and 'what is below forms' has a slight resemblance to the distinction between metaphysics and physics, but it is more specific.

The one who 'assumes' or 'hypothesises' can be called a genius. But a genius steps into the language-world trap more readily, and, in a way more foolishly, than ordinary people.

He often ends up fettered to an imagined pillar of language, but assumes he is in the real world.

Genius is a unique type of activity in the mind. By means of 'assuming', it constantly sends appearances in the mind adrift.

Genius is the capability to identify certain skandhas that have been assembled in the mind.

In the drifting process of skandhas, connotations of genius are represented as connotations of language. Genius, as a skandha with insights, can be represented in appearances, or a flow of mantra.

A mantra needs to be chanted rather than understood. It is a most primitive and mysterious way of speaking.

A mantra is not meant to reveal thoughts, but to eliminate thoughts. It is thinking–perceiving.

As Wittgenstein puts it:

> There is no more light in a genius than in any other honest human being — but the genius concentrates this light into a burning point by means of a particular kind of lens.

And:

> Why is the soul moved by idle thoughts – since, they are after all, idle? Well, it is moved by them.

(How can the wind move a tree, since it is after all, just wind? Well, it does move it; and don't forget it.)[74]

Language is not wind, but wind can be used as a metaphor to refer to language.

A poetic way of speaking is a figurative tool of language. Swaying along with metaphors, it moves like waves, but remains silent, like a flower.

In language, as well as in the mind, a common appearance or 'uniting element' does not exist that is 'not birth or destruction, purity or defilement, completeness or deficiency'. This proposition by the *Heart Sutra*, somehow contradictory to the doctrine of emptiness, should be a proposition by Thales or Plato rather than by the Buddha. Therefore, in relation to emptiness adrift being the 'noumenon' of Buddhist teachings, this line can be marked as a flaw in the writing of the *Heart Sutra*, for it indicates the intrinsic existence of a personified deity (the Buddha in the theistic sense, or, God) in the Buddhist philosophical system. Buddhist teachings show clearly that the Buddha himself utterly denies the existence of such a personified God representing totality or universal essence.

On the other hand, a theistic Buddha – the 'common appearance' – is necessary for believers of the religious system of Buddhism. The line might, therefore, be regarded as an

---

74 *Translator's Note:* The English version is from: Wittgenstein, Ludwig, *Culture and Value: A Selection from the Posthumous Remains*, edited by Georg Henrik von Wright, translated by Peter Winch, Blackwell Publishers, 1998.

advance hint from the past, whereby the author of the *Heart Sutra* foreshadows the future development of Buddhism.

There indeed hangs a ladder between humanity and God, for which the Buddha has no use, but which is necessary for human beings.

Put simply, the Dharma (Buddhist teaching) is a particularity-oriented speaking system focusing on specific appearances, whereas Buddhism (the religion) is a universality-oriented speaking system focusing on common appearance.

The Dharma teaches ways for humanity to realise enlightenment; it is the path leading to personal salvation and nirvana. Buddhism puts deities in control of all matters; it represents the submission of human beings to deities – mostly for the sake of seeking or receiving blessings.

Within the framework of Language Drift Theory, language traverses both common appearance and particular appearances, carrying with it 'emptiness' and 'existence', while at the same time unceasingly generating 'emptiness' and 'existence'.

Speaking, when confronted with the problem of not being able to put something into words, can do nothing but mantra chanting to release tension. Through chanting, semantic meaning adrift is transformed into vocal rhythms, as in 'the mantra in Prajnaparamita spoken thus: *"Gate gate, paragate, parasangate, bodhi svaha"*.'

The mantra guides the heart just as stars illuminate the night sky. Go ahead, go ahead; go to realise enlightenment; go to practice, to achieve nirvana.

There is, in fact, no point in 'going' anywhere, except for going ahead, sending skandhas in the mind adrift. There is no destination for 'going'; drifting of skandhas is, in itself, the destination.

A poem titled 'Refuge', from my *Shangrila* poetry series, attempts to encapsulate this:

> To seek refuge within a poem,
>   is my ultimate conclusion
> To seek refuge within a feast of Spring's catkins,
>   will be the testament to my wilting
> Oh, Spring!
>   The lily does not know the blue of the empty sky
> Upon the earth, a sea of lilies drifting in the night,
>   above which rises only a crescent moon
> In the distance, lilies, gathering like the ears of ermines,
>   are crossing the bellows of hoarfrost
> Oh, Spring!
>   What of the pink rust of that year's lilies?
>   What of the thimbles in their buds?
>
>   (Translated by Thomas Garbarini)

Enjoying Leisure Time (#18). Album leaf, ink on paper, 17.5 x 22.8 cm, by Dan Dang.

Chapter eleven

The way the Five Skandhas Exist

The Five Skandhas, also called the Five Aggregates, consist of form (*rupa*), sensation *(vedana)*, perception *(sanjna)*, memory *(sanskara)* and consciousness *(vijnana)*. They represent five means for us to interact with the world. Together, by way of drifting, the Five Skandhas become the one skandha of emptiness. Hence, 'they were empty of self-existence'.

The Buddha, in an attempt to attain the true essence of existence, made an effort to dissolve the duality between the outside and inside worlds by mending the gap between the two. It proved futile, however. The World Honoured One[75] realised, perhaps just at the moment he seemed about to attain his lofty aspiration, that the true essence was impossible to grasp. He consequently felt utter disappointment, and even fear.

But the Buddha, in his greatness, turned this disappointment, or fear, into joy; and transformed the helpless mind into the joyful mind. From this perspective, bodhisattvas, meaning 'awakened sentient beings', offer salvation; and *anuttara-samyak-sambodhi*, meaning 'unexcelled complete enlightenment', offers the ultimate salvation.

Bill Porter observes:

> Basically the skandhas represent an attempt to exhaust the possible paths we might take in our search for a self, for something permanent or pure or sepa-

---

75 *Translator's Note*: This is one of the titles of Shakyamuni Buddha in Buddhist sutras. Other titles for the Buddha include, for instance, the One That Has Come (or, Thus Come One), Well Departed, the Englishtened One and the Awakened One.

rate in the undifferentiated flux of experience. They are five ways of considering our world and looking for something we can call our own. This is why Avalokiteshvara looks upon the Five Skandhas. The Five Skandhas are the limit of reality. If we are going to find anything real, this is where we are going to find it. But no matter how often or how long or how intently we search through the skandhas, we come up empty-handed. Thus, the skandha of form is often compared to foam, because it cannot be grasped; the skandha of sensation to a bubble, because it lasts but an instant; the skandha of perception to a mirage, because it only appears to exist; the skandha of memory to a banana tree, because it has no core; and the skandha of consciousness to an illusion, because it is a well-concealed deception. And yet the skandhas are not separate from what is real.

(Bill Porter, p. 71)

To acknowledge the significance of each individual skandha while emphasising their common 'emptiness' is indeed to attempt the impossible. It is similar to the striving of individual human beings, with vital sensory and perceptual systems, to develop a transcendental grasp of the cosmos (the material world) in which they exist.

Humans exist in the cosmos as roundworms do in human intestines. Roundworms, as a life form, may perhaps sense the existence of an outer cosmos called 'human', but they are never able to view this cosmos as a whole. Of course, humans, being far more intelligent than roundworms, are capable of perceiving the outside world through synthesising and analysing what they have directly sensed through their sensory system. One may doubt, however, how reliable their perception or sense is, and this doubt becomes the departure point of thinking–perceiving.

In fact, the comparatively more complex sensory and perceptual system of human beings might be what distinguishes them from other life forms – after all, humans have long acknowledged this complexity as the source of their exceptional intelligence, based on which they have proudly claimed themselves the 'wisest of all creation'.

Through their perceptual system, human beings are capable of synthesising and analysing what they sense in the outside world, and, furthermore, capable of creating concepts, which, in the form of skandhas, provide approaches for making sense of the outside world. Moreover, their ability to invent tools enables them to expand the material world into one of knowledge, tools and poetry. But the paradox is: in their very attempt to create concepts or approaches for elucidating the essence of the world or cosmos, human beings find themselves moving further away from the world they have created through 'speaking', and further away from the essence of existence, which may ultimately be known only to the cosmos itself. For instance, metaphysics and mathematics, which humans have created, are precisely where absurdity begins in the eyes of philosophers like Wittgenstein.

Though the Buddha did speak about the world with help of the Five Skandhas, he was cautious in making use of concepts (in this case, skandhas) throughout the history of metaphysics; for, as he resorts to concepts, he at the same time dissolves them. This plainly exhibits the Buddha's unsurpassed wisdom and perfection of enlightened practice, which is bound to endure through the ages, and has special resonance for today's world, in which creation of concepts, false propositions and logical fallacies have made existence feel absurd, and dehumanised people.

The following two verses from my *Orange in Field* poetry series, originally dedicated to Plato, are now re-dedicate to the Buddha.

1
Where is that ocean?
You once used its water
To scrawl the first full moon
Where is that sky?
You gave it, singularity, purity
You once set an orange tune to the crescent moon
And then, erased it with your own hand

2
From within the looking glass
You released the sun from its shackles
Letting it ascend, lithe and graceful
And you controlled it, just right
So it could neither soar, nor sunder

(Translated by Thomas Garbarini)

The drifting of skandhas is, by nature, poetic and, therefore, anti-logic.

Though the concepts of the Five Skandhas manage to achieve self-liberation in the drifting process, their individual conceptual meaning remains uncertain, for, through drifting, it comes to be; and through drifting, it ceases to be. Wittgenstein once observed in *Culture and Value* that: 'Human beings can regard all the evil within them as illusions (or, blindness).' Likewise, we might imagine that human beings can also regard all good deeds and all thoughts as illusions. Reality and illusions both exist in the mind; together they form the poetically mysterious manner in which the human sensory experience of life and perceptual system exist.

A person whose mind consists exclusively of reality qualifies to be called no other than 'matter'. How fearful it would be for the mind to be composed of only matter!

A beautiful mind is, without exception, filled with illusion-like reality and reality-like illusions; it is immersed in a wondrous state characterised by sacredness and poeticness of faith and dream.

As Wittgenstein puts it:

> My thoughts probably move in a far narrower circle than I suspect!
>
> Thoughts rise to the surface slowly, like bubbles.
>
> Sometimes it's as though you could see a thought, an idea, as an indistinct point far away on

the horizon; and then it often comes closer with surprising speed.[76]

The Five Skandhas in the *Heart Sutra* might be regarded as five types of illusion. All real things or actions are none other than illusions or false appearances created by language.

And reality at the level of language is illusory. Whether it becomes real depends on whether or not you believe it. If you do, it becomes part of you and part of the world.

Bishop George Berkeley[77] famously claimed, 'to be is to be perceived'. To him, time as well as space is perceived reality rather than permanent existence. Therefore, reality is no other than the mind; it consists exclusively of minds and their ideas.

The Five Skandhas are the five petals of the flower of mind.

Rather than referring to any particular skandha, each of the Five Skandhas stands for one category of skandha; each category generates limitless further skandhas.

The forms of skandhas, as well as their meanings, remain in constant flux and transformation. Typically, for instance, a dead mind is composed exclusively of dead skandhas.

---

76 *Translator's Note:* The English version is from: Ludwig Wittgenstein, *Culture and Value*, Blackwell Publishers, 1998.

77 *Translator's Note:* Bishop George Berkeley (1685–1753) was an Irish philosopher of the Age of Enlightenment, best known for his theory of Immaterialism, a type of Idealism (he is sometimes considered the father of modern Idealism). Along with John Locke and David Hume, he is also a major figure in the British Empiricism movement.

Every mind consists of such a five-petalled flower; every such flower opens and unfolds itself in a unique manner at the moment of its momentary existence.

Enjoying Leisure Time (#21). Album leaf, ink on paper, 17.5 x 22.8 cm, by Dan Dang.

Chapter twelve

Rupa-Skandha is the 'Line in the Magic Horn'

Existence and non-existence depend on each other; in constant flux, they are represented by the never-ending dependent arising of appearances, both in the universe and in the mind. Appearances in the mind are what we call skandhas; their occurence and passing away is dependent. And whether in the realm of existence or non-existence (which are both defined by emptiness), *rupa*-skandha, the Skandha of Form, is the first skandha that the sensory system actualises in substantiating the external world.

Rupa implies the action to look. Form is *rupa*, and the absence of *rupa* means the absence of form.

Rupa implies to look with both the eyes and the mind.

The things being looked at and the means of looking, together, form the impression of the world that one has experienced. A door seen by someone at a certain angle is *rupa*-skandha in the form of an individual door; but it can also be *rupa*-skandha as a category (of doors). Thus, the concept of *rupa*-skandha drifts from specific appearances to category-appearance, and vice versa. It is worth noting that specific appearances are what appear to be, whereas category-appearance, as a superordinate concept, represents what lies behind specific appearances.

The various kinds of form (of objects or of the mind) reveal how *rupa*-skandha drifts in different ways. In other words, the form as well as the meaning of *rupa*-skandha does not remain unchanged but undergoes continuous transformation; it represents the norm of existence of the dharmas – that is, impermanence marked by continuous dependent arising and passing away. Throughout this process, both poetic forms and non-poetic forms are generated; they interdepend, inter-drift, and interact to achieve manifestation.

Rupa can be something real in the material world, or conceptual categories drifting in the mind. In either case, the concept of *rupa* is substantiated into a certain illusory form, and thus obtains a poetic, momentary existence. In fact, poetry is generated when various types of form evolve and go adrift. Thus, in the following untitled poem by Li Shangyin, rich literary imagery is produced, when various types of form – external objects and internal emotions – are depicted.

Last night's stars, last night's wind,
  West of the painted house, east of the cassia hall.
Our bodies have no colourful phoenix-wings to fly side by side,
  Our hearts are linked by the line in the magic horn[78].
From seat to seat the hook is passed, the spring wine is warm,
  Under the red candle's light
we guess at riddles in divided teams.
Alas, when the drum sounded I had to answer duty's call,
  I ride my horse to Orchid Terrace as tumbleweed in the wind.

                   (Translated by Emily Bowden)[79]

'Something real' means what exists in the form of matter, a functional object or an event. It is called matter, for

---

78 *Translator's Note:* The 'horn' in this poem refers to a magical rhinoceros horn. According to Chinese legend, telepathic powers can be conferred through the white line in a rhinoceros horn. This line of the poem has become a well-known idiom (*xin you ling xi yi dian tong*, 心有灵犀一点通), implying a meeting of minds, or two hearts that beat as one, with mutual sensitivity or tacit romantic feeling.

79 *Translator's Note:* The English translation of the poem is from: Emily Bowden, *A Failure to Communicate*: Li Shangyin's *Hermetic Legacy*, unpublished master's thesis, University of Kansas. 2015.

example, in the case of the matter of a 'table-form'. But the table-form matter becomes an object with an allotted function, namely, a 'desk', when it is placed in a classroom. People often misconstrue matter as the same as existence or essence of being, but matter is merely one form in which things exist. Apart from material being, things also exist in other forms, including functional being, metaphorical being, symbolic being, etc. For example, when the same table is put on a platform, it becomes a 'podium', with a changed function. Though the matter of the table is the same, it is now metaphorically associated with power or superiority, and symbolically implies an authoritative position, located high above others sitting below. The changed name results in a changed representation of *rupa*.

When *rupa*-skandha, or the Skandha of Form, momentarily exists in different appearances, its function goes adrift. When the function goes adrift, *rupa*-skandha comes into momentary existence. With the skandha's drifting, the mind also drifts.

Therefore, *rupa*-skandha can be understood as form–appearances in either momentary existence or a drifting state. The Chinese for *rupa* is *se*, which literally means 'colour', but *rupa* is actually more than colour. Colour is linked to only one of the five senses (the sight), and can be seen as drifting form–colour in momentary existence.

All appearances, whether real or unreal, exist as some kind of form–appearance. And without form–colour, there is no appearance. For example, we decide whether a student is present in a class based on the presence of his shape and appearance, rather than on the presence of his mind. Shape combined with appearance makes up what we call *rupa*, or form, and the sense of sight plays a central role in experiencing *rupa*, though all other senses might also play a part. For instance, the sense of smell, apart from the sense of sight, may contribute to the judgement that 'an ox is present in the classroom'.

A poem of mine titled 'Winter Clouds' depicts the inter-connection of various kinds of form:

> In winter when the clouds panic
>   I want your sanctuary
> My little Muse, I want the silver needle of the void sky
>   pressing down upon the freshet of Green Lake
> Withstanding the blight of light and shade
>   amidst the despair of a million wind-blown lamps
> In winter under the iron gears of a locomotive
>   I want your sanctuary
> My little Muse, I want to resist the cold ash in the void sky
>   I want all of the leaking oceans and
> anchored peaks to vomit sawdust
>
>   (Translated by Thomas Garbarini)

The world we 'see' with our eyes is, in fact, one with *rupa*-skandha drifting about. We can stay ignorant of what profound meaning this world holds, but human instinct should drive us to explore how it comes to be conceived in our conceptual system. Apparently it gets shaped in the mind, above all, via the sense of sight. But even someone born blind experiences the external world based on an invisible kind of *rupa*, or form – through the sense of touch and the sense of hearing. In short, we become aware of the world around us primarily based on the sense of sight, which, supported by other senses, helps establish the conceptual category of form. That is why the first skandha among the Five Skandhas is the Skandha of Form.

Master Deqing, one of the great Buddhist monks of the Ming period (1368–1644), said, 'Form is the physical existence of humans. Ordinary people suffer from attachment to it because they consider their physical bodies to be real, something that they have possession of. It represents the essence of man's deep-rooted illusions and is thus the attachment that is most difficult to abandon.' Indeed, while form does refer to man's physical existence, at the same time it should be considered not as man's physical existence.

Master Zhixu, another great Buddhist monk of the Ming period, made it even clearer, saying:

It is clear that form is nothing but the mind; apart from the mind, there is no real form. All things, including the abodes, bodies, objects, and realms, are but delusions like dreams. Thus it says, 'form is not separate from emptiness'. But even emptiness is nothing but the mind; apart from the mind, there is no emptiness. Suppose there exists a dharma that surpasses nirvana, it should also be seen as illusory, like dreams. Thus it says, 'emptiness is not separate from form'. If they are not separate from each other, they are the same. It is indeed insightful of Zhixu to view the Five Skandhas as 'nothing but the mind'.[80]

---

80 *Author's Note:* Both this quotation of Master Zhixu and the quotation of Master Deqing are from: *The Prajnaparamita Heart Sutra: A Variorium Edition,* The Corporate Body of the Buddha Educational Foundation, 2001.

Master Hongyi,[81] the pre-eminent Chinese artist–monk of the twentieth century, points out that the Skandha of Form connotes 'obstruction'.[82] Note that 'obstruction' is used in this context as a neutral word, referring to the contact between sensual faculty and sense objects, which results in the sensual faculty's being disturbed or activated. Interestingly, the neutral word 'wall' is similarly often used metaphorically to mean 'obstruction', or 'disturbance', to the mind. Of course, obstruction not only exists in the mind; it represents the original state of the mind, for there is no mind that is completely free from disturbance.

As I see it, form is what is visible to the eyes without obstruction. It originates in the mind's desire to 'look', manifests itself through material objects, and is eventually perceived by the mind as being 'seen'. For example, you take the initiative to 'look', and the house in front of your eyes 'obstructs' or 'disturbs' your vision, hindering you from seeing what lies behind it. The house, by becoming a 'disturbance', manifests itself to you. In other words, 'looking' in itself is not only a manifestation of appearances; it is also the means by which appearances are manifested. Manifestation of this kind, by presenting to the eyes what is looked upon, is free from any 'disturbance' of the metaphorical sense, and represents the visible way the Skandha of Form exists.

---

81 *Translator's Note:* Master Hongyi (1880–1942), born Li Shutong, is a well-known Chinese Buddhist monk, artist and art teacher.

82 *Author's Note:* All direct or indirect quotations from Master Hongyi in this book are from: *Complete Works of Master Hongyi*, Volume 1, *Essays in Buddhism,* Fujian People's Publishing House, 1991.

The act of looking results in the aggregation of form (*rupa*), which is then conceived by the mind. The sky perceived in your mind is form aggregated from the sky in your act of looking; likewise, the Earth perceived in your mind is form aggregated from the Earth in your act of looking.

Therefore, the Skandha of Form is, to me, 'appreciable appearance' – appearance readily perceived by the senses – that consists of real, unreal and illusory appearances. It is, above all, appearance in the mind.

Form readily perceived by the senses is in effect the self-manifestation of objects or events; and 'appreciable appearance' in its self-manifestation is liable to generate 'appreciable appearances' in a deeper sense.

The illusion of 'appreciable appearance' is not necessarily real or unreal, but is more likely a combination of the two. For example; the audio-visual manifestations of art are neither real nor unreal, but should be viewed as a kind of 'inappreciable appearance' that is transformed from 'appreciable appearance', as a result of stimulated artistic expression.

The appearance of abstract art may be either appreciable or opaque, but either way marks the temporary dwelling of appearances in the mind.

Even hyper-realist paintings, if viewed from the perspective of drifting skandhas, may turn out to be no other than appreciable or opaque appearance of delusions. For, in a poetic sense, deep beneath the most realist artistic work lies, perhaps, the most abstract, indescribable spirit.

Form in the appreciable sense is not concerned with what style, whether realist or abstract, it is labelled with. It is only concerned about manifesting itself in the most accurate and obvious manner through 'appreciable appearance'.

For instance, trees may be presented in very different styles: for example, the oak trees of the Russian Peredvizhniki (Itinerant) painter Ivan Shishkin, *Red Tree* by Dutch painter Piet Mondrian, or *Walnut Trees* by contemporary British painter David Hockney. They all, however, represent the 'appreciable appearance' of trees. Irrespective of whether the trees are painted with lines or colour blocks, form is successfully manifestated as 'appreciable appearance'. In fact, truly great works must be explicit and sincere in expressing 'appreciable appearance', for only then can poetic spirit be represented.

It does not matter whether trees exist as illusory, real or unreal appearances; whether they appear in the sky, on the Earth, or in dreams; whether they are portrayed with a perspective view, or painted with flatly; whether they appear as shapes of trees, or as tree collages; whether they are depicted in a representational or abstract style. All these kinds of tree are form in the mind, symbolic expressions of temporary existence. The same is true for all other things in the universe.

'Appreciable appearance', when sent adrift, is transformed into 'opaque appearance'; and the latter, when coming into temporary existence at a specific locus in the drifting, is again transformed into 'appreciable appearance'.

All appearances are empty. The statement, 'form is emptiness' implies that form bears no extra adhering or concealed meaning apart from its original material features, and that form is defined by emptiness through the act of drifting – after all, an object in itself without being perceived in the realm of form is not capable of drifting.

Were form to be defined by stability, it would not be capable of drifting; and appearances not capable of drifting are dead.

Some people live with dead skandhas of the mind; some others, though physically dead, leave behind skandhas of the mind that last forever.

The living mind is a drifting skandha that exists free from the bondage of life. It is what has enabled civilisations, cultures and poetry to pass on through generations.

The mind is dead where skandhas have ceased drifting.

The poet whose physical body has long ceased to be continues to live, if his poetry continues to drift along to shape the mind. For instance, in reading the following ci^{83} poem by Xin Qiji, and sharing his feelings, I, a reader from the 21st century, and the poet, who lived during the Southern Song

---

83 *Translator's Note: Ci* is a genre of Chinese poetry characterised by lines of unequal length with prescribed rhyme schemes and tonal patterns. To compose a *ci*, a poet would typically choose from a set of about eight hundred traditional tunes (*cipai*) and insert his own unique words to fit the rhythm and meter. For this *ci* poem by Xin Qiji, 'Blessing the Groom' is a the title of the traditional tune, whereas 'How Feeble I've Become' is the title added by the poet.

period eight hundred years ago, become connected as one. The poem, 'How Feeble I've Become', is written to the tune of 'Blessing the Groom':

> Oh, how feeble I've become! I rue this life – my companions, save but a few, have scattered to the winds, and all I have is my long white mane and my derision of worldly affairs. What is it, then, that can enliven me? That wooded mountain appears jaunty and at ease; and the mountain, I believe, thinks the same of me. In feeling and in form, we are quite alike.
>
> Sipping wine in remembrance before the eastern window; this must be how Tao Yuanming felt when he penned 'Lingering Clouds'. Those drunkards in the south pining for fame – good wine is lost on them. Spinning around, my song calls a tempest into being. I do not lament that I will never meet the great men of yore; I lament that they will never hear my wild verse. Who truly knows me? I can name but a handful.
>
> (Translated by Thomas Garbarini)

Enjoying Leisure Time (#22). Album leaf, ink on paper, 17.5 x 22.8 cm, by Dan Dang.

Chapter thirteen

The Tidal Force of Spiritual Liberation

Every single element of language contributes to the tidal force of spiritual liberation (*paramita*).

Paramita literally means 'reaching the Other Shore', implying an act of 'crossing over', and a path or ferry for crossing. It represents the mysterious drifting journey of a raft, which, after numerous twists and turns, manages to arrive at the glorious land of enlightenment. It is a journey that liberates the practitioner from all suffering, and, since suffering is an innate part of the mind, it can only be effectively dealt with in the mind. Where suffering ends, the realm of emptiness, or nirvana, arrives.

Therefore, *paramita* should be considered a skandha, which, if understood from the perspective of Language Drift Theory, means guide, save, enlighten or call upon. It brings into being a brand new time and space, and helps generate all drifting appearances, as it successfully guides the mind through all obstructions and suffering. As the chant goes, '[T]hat wooded mountain appears jaunty and at ease; and the mountain, I believe, thinks the same of me. In feeling and in form, we are quite alike.' Here, the mountain functions as *paramita* in liberating the chanter's soul.

Emptiness marks the very original state when the ten thousand appearances are sent adrift in the mind; it also defines the drifting process and destination. Emptiness is, virtually, the mother of appearance, and it is in the realm of emptiness that *paramita* sets appearances in motion. In a sense, emptiness is a force, or energy, that promises a boundless range of possibilities for the ten thousand appearances to develop.

At a certain moment in the drifting, emptiness and *paramita* become merged into one.

Paramita serves as a bridge with no physical bridge in sight; operates as a paddle with no tangible paddle at hand; and functions as a raft with no real raft to board. It works along with emptiness and other skandhas, surges forward like a rushing tidal wave at sea, until it reaches non-existence, from which existence arises and to which it returns.

Paramita is located at the 'mid-point' between the two extremes of existence and non-existence. It represents an energy conversion resulting from a harmonious collaboration between language and wisdom.

Through drifting, *paramita* not only 'heals all suffering', but also 'heals all joy', since joy, essentially, is no different from suffering. Suffering and joy are like yin and yang – the two poles of the Way (Dao or Tao), which both complement each other and oppose each other. Suffering of the highest degree lies in the pain of seeking meaning for life; and pain of the highest level lies no more in death than in life. Life and death are both skandhas that are 'thrown into' the world, whereas *paramita*, by providing a spiritual path, ferries across to the Other Shore all the phenomena that are involved: life, death, and all the twists and turns between the two.

The liberation of an individual usually results in a single mind going adrift, but in some circumstances, this single liberated mind may bring liberation to all human beings, causing all minds to be sent adrift. As Karen Armstrong, British commentator on Comparative Religion, observes:

Gotama [Siddhartha Gautama] felt that his life had become meaningless. A conviction that the world was awry was fundamental to the spirituality that emerged in the Axial countries. Those who took part in this transformation felt restless – just as Gotama did. They were consumed by a sense of helplessness, were obsessed by their mortality and felt a profound terror of and alienation from the world. They expressed this malaise in different ways. The Greeks saw life as a tragic epic, a drama in which they strove for *katharsis* and release. Plato spoke of man's separation from the divine, and yearned to cast off the impurity of our present state and achieve unity with the Good. The Hebrew prophets of the eighth, seventh and sixth centuries felt a similar alienation from God, and saw their political exile as symbolic of their spiritual condition. The Zoroastrians of Iran saw life as a cosmic battle between Good and Evil, while in China, Confucius lamented the darkness of his age, which had fallen away from the ideals of the ancestors. In India, Gotama and the forest monks were convinced that life was *dukkha*: it was fundamentally wry', filled with pain, grief and sorrow. The world had become a frightening place. The Buddhist scriptures speak of the 'terror, awe and dread' that people experienced when they ventured outside the city and went into the woods. Nature had become obscurely menacing, rather as it had become inimical to Adam and Eve after their lapse. Gotama did not leave home to commune happily with nature in the woods, but experienced a continuous 'fear and horror'. If a deer approached or if the wind rustled in the leaves, he recalled later, his hair stood on end.[84]

Siddhartha Gautama clearly encountered the difficulties of life – spiritual suffering and spiritual responsibilities, but he did not evade them. Rather, as Karen Armstrong points out, 'In leaving home...Gotama [Gautama] was not abjuring the modern world for a more traditional or even archaic lifestyle (as monks are often perceived to be doing today), but was in the vanguard of change.' (p. 63). Those who have long practised Buddhism would share this understanding of life, which might prove to exert an even more powerful influence today than ever before, now that the depravity of the human spirit has reached new levels.

Certainly, the Dharma is a great 'philosophy of action', teaching joy, or bliss. But it should be noted that this 'philosophy of action' is not so named just for the sake of naming. That is to say, Buddhist philosophy is not concept-oriented, as Western mainstream philosophy is; rather, it is *paramita*-oriented, seeking to transcend concepts by putting into practice, in the mind, the propositions of action philosophy. To be more specific, Buddhist philosophy is intent on liberating the mind, or, sending the mind adrift, rather than superficially enquiring about what constitutes the universe – whether it is life, soul, spiritual monads (in Gottfried Leibniz's words), or other conceptual things. Therefore, *parami-*

---

84 *Translator's Note:* Karen Armstrong, *The Buddha*, Penguin (Non-Classics), 2004, pp. 43–4.

ta is not merely a name, or a concept, but a linguistic form in motion that the philosopher resorts to; or a driving force of soul that can be represented in no other way except through language. Ultimately, even these names and concepts are to be dispensed with by the Buddhadharma, for, 'the so-called buddhas and dharmas are not real buddhas and dharmas' – this amazing insight of Buddhist philosophy represents the greatest idea in linguistic philosophy. From this perspective, Buddhist philosophy can be considered non-philosophy and anti-philosophy. Alain Badiou elaborated on the question of names as follows,

> Wittgenstein does not clarify this question of names, which has been the topic of strong debates in philosophy since at least The Cratylus. I can certainly understand that in the proposition names represent objects combined in the state of affairs, described by the proposition in which these names appear. But what I do not understand is how the unthinkable difference of objects comes to be represented by the difference attested to by the names. Here, a fissure slips into the specular construction that brings face-to-face the multiple of objects (on the side of substance) and the multiple of names (on the side of the proposition, or of the picture). If objects violate the Leibnizian principle of indiscernibles, how is it that names, which are there only as signs of objects, obey this principle? Because it is certain, no matter what the extent of homonymy might be, that two indiscernible names ultimately are the same. Names, as opposed to objects, are

not identified by their external relations. They have a dense intrinsic identity.[85]

Alain Badiou seeks to connect objects to propositions with the help of poetry, hoping to break down the barriers between the two and realise freedom of thought. This, in my view, rightly serves the purpose of '*paramita*', or, 'crossing over'. Of course, opposite to my assertion, Alain Badiou regards poetry as a thought, whereas I believe that poetry is simply the means by which the poetic spirit manifests itself. Though the poetic spirit co-exists with the poetic form, it is by no means the thought itself. *Paramita*, in my opinion, manifests the poetic spirit in the broad sense, and is thus certainly different from the 'thought as a practice of language' proposed by Alain Badiou. In the matrix of the mind, language functions as the original force of '*paramita*', but only poetic language is capable of breaking down the barriers between names and objects, and bridging the gap between the two. In other words, poetic imagery, though by nature no other than 'dreams, illusions, bubbles, or shadows', is still the most effective and penetrating in serving the purpose of '*paramita*'.

Do events exist in isolation from each other? Are the 'simple substances' of things truly isolated existence? In discussing Gottfried Leibniz's theory that monads form a unity of the ordered universe with a universal harmony and thus proves the existence of God, historians of philosophy put it as follows:

---

[85] *Translator's Note:* Alain Badiou, *Wittgenstein's Antiphilosophy*, Verso, 2011, p. 108

Each monad behaves in accordance with its own created purpose. These *windowless* monads, each following its own purpose, form a unity of the ordered universe. Even though each is isolated from the other, their separate purposes form a large-scale harmony. It is as though several clocks all struck the same hour because they keep perfect time. Leibniz compares all these monads to several different bands of musicians and choirs, playing their parts separately; and so placed that they do not see or even hear one another. Nevertheless, Leibniz continues, they keep perfectly together, by each following their own notes, in such a way that he who hears them all finds in them a harmony that is wonderful, and much more surprising than if there had been any connection between them. Each monad, then, is a separate world, but all the activities of each monad occur in harmony with the activities of the others. In this way we can say that each monad mirrors the whole universe but from a unique perspective.[86]

In presupposing an Absolute Unity (God) as the origin of harmony, Leibniz's idea clearly stems from an ancient speculation of Rationalism – though, unlike Plato, who based his arguments on assumptions, Leibniz appears to have great confidence in his proclamations. He was unaware that the poetic creativity behind the 'harmony' he describes lies precisely in the poetical and spiritual communication between

---

[86] *Translator's Note:* Samuel Enoch Stumpf & James Fieser, *Socrates to Sartre and Beyond: A History of Philosophy*, McGraw-Hill, 2007, p. 223

the monads he presumes isolated. The Buddha, in contrast, considers everything to be in flux, and therefore, annihilates the existence of a prior cause (an eternal unity). To the Buddha, everything exists in a series of dependently arising links, hence, dependent arising is emptiness and emptiness is dependent arising. This insight of the Buddha is, perhaps, the most accurate and reliable description of the existence of the external physical world and the internal mental universe, and is in fact the very origin of my Language Drift Theory.

Of course, harmony would be impossible to achieve without the temporary dwelling of poetry, which features both constant transformation and explicit revelation. Because harmony is essentially the intuitive perception of life, which is manifested in poetical drifting, temporary dwelling and transformation.

Harmony as the ideal of beauty represents the supreme principle of poetics in Western traditions. But from the perspective of Language Drift Theory, there exist no such things as determinism, ontology or aesthetics. Harmony is viewed as the representation of a certain skandha; and all skandhas are represented for the sake of *paramita*, or for the purpose of spiritual liberation. Therefore, harmony is also a skandha in a drifting state; otherwise it would be as dead as those aesthetic concepts. *Paramita* in driftage and the drifting of *paramita*, conceived from this perspective, are immediately endowed with the ineffable beauty of poetry. A poem titled 'Swimming Fish' from my *House* series depicts the bliss of *paramita*.

Bring your scales,
   bring the capitulation of the waves.
Bring your eyes,
   bring the boredom of the vast ocean.
Bring your wagging tails,
   bring the square matrix of your fins, ancient painted masks.
Who is urging? It is me.
   I cleanse rhetoric with your full, rounded mouths.
I have a ravine for you to come out to sea.
   I have a mesa for you to ascend, against the current.
I have the corner of a drum for you to hear.
   I erect a sail and wipe away a shadow for you to contend.

(Translated by Thomas Garbarini)

Enjoying Leisure Time (#23). Album leaf, ink on paper, 17.5 x 22.8 cm, by Dan Dang.

Chapter fourteen

The Form–Emptiness Wheel

'Form is emptiness, emptiness is form. Emptiness is not separate from form, form is not separate from emptiness'. This statement describes the inter-relationship between form and emptiness as a metaphorical whirling wheel of form and emptiness, or a spinning circle of the mind that draws in the other four skandhas. The wheel is both round and flat, for the circle spins only in a metaphorical sense. Ultimately, this metaphorical form–emptiness wheel whirls with all Five Skandhas drawn into its whirling emptiness.

Indeed, the mind of the enlightened Buddha is a structure represented by the form–emptiness wheel. If the mind is a form–emptiness wheel, so is the physical being of humans. When the form–emptiness wheel whirls, it is in fact skandhas that are whirling.

Of course, when this form–emptiness wheel of humanity whirls, it is for the purpose of breaking free, first and foremost, from attachment to the self; then from attachment to others; and eventually from attachment to the very concept of 'self' and 'other'. Attachment to the self, others, and the concept of 'self' and 'other' comprises the basic foundation of both culture and humanity. When Gautama surpassed the limit of ordinary human beings and attained enlightenment, he was actually returning to *chuxin* (an open beginner's state of mind) and an original 'humanhood'. Human beings – both individuals and humanity as a whole – have gone further and further on the path toward 'non-humanhood', but Buddhist practice provides a way to reverse this tendency. By sending the form–emptiness wheel whirling, it brings the restored mind to a mysterious dreamland, where the mind and things unfold. As the *Shurangama Sutra* describes, 'All the things that exist in the world are the wonderfully bright inherent mind of bodhi. The essence of mind is completely pervading and contains the ten directions.'

The 'wonderfully bright inherent mind' cannot be attained until, in the process of whirling, the self achieves purification and salvation by getting rid of Mara, the shadow-self. Karen Armstrong writes in *The Buddha*:

> Mara, Gotama's [Gautama's] shadow-self, appeared before him, decked out like a cakkavatti, a World Ruler, with a massive army. Mara himself was mounted on an elephant that was 150 leagues high. He had sprouted 1,000 arms, each of which brandished a deadly weapon. Mara's name means 'delusion'. He epitomised the ignorance which holds us back from enlightenment.

In this allegory, which describes how the Buddha defeated Mara, his shadow-self, both *cakkavatti* and the massive army represent Mara. Once Gautama won the fight against Mara, namely, the self, his form–emptiness wheel whirled its way into a bright and pure land of the mind:

> Now Gotama [Gautama] entered the first *jhana* and penetrated the inner world of his psyche; when he finally reached the peace of Nibbana all the worlds of the Buddhist cosmos were convulsed, the heavens and hells shook, and the bodhi tree rained down red

florets on the enlightened man. Throughout all the worlds, *the flowering trees bloomed; the fruit trees were weighed down by the burden of their fruit; the trunk lotuses bloomed on the trunks of trees.... The system of ten thousand worlds was like a bouquet of flowers sent whirling through the air.*[87]

This again is an allegory about how Gautama attained enlightenment, and like many other allegories on this theme, it is written in a verse form – implying that poetry plays a role in sending the form–emptiness wheel of the enlightened ones whirling.

The form–emptiness wheel turns, but there are no theories rotating with it. The turning of the wheel does not represent a 'changing of the guard' for the protective energies in the watchtowers that flank the heart. In fact, in the turning of the form–emptiness wheel, there are no either-or binary definitions, principles, methods or ideologies. In the moment that the wheel turns, all theories are rendered utterly impotent. After all, the Dharma is ineffable; it fails all language, but is accessible only when it 'spills over' from the secret, meaningless form–emptiness domain. Such spillover is both cause and effect; it is the bodhi blossom enjoying total freedom.

Readers might look to my *Early Spring* series, where there is a poem titled 'Cherry':

---

87 *Translator's Note:* Karen Armstrong, The Buddha, Penguin (Non-Classics), 2004, p. 139–42.

> The cherry branch's solitude spills over
> > Redness on treetips
> A tree's solitude spills over
> > Growing into cherries
> The earth's solitude spills over
> > Raising up trees
> Spring's solitude spills over
> > Across a thousand leagues of crowing roosters

(Translated by Nick Rosenbaum)

Rotating in the whirling form–emptiness wheel there is no so-called essence, but only language, whose 'essence of mind is completely pervading and contains the ten directions'. It does not, however, dwell for long, otherwise appearances might get defiled,[88] and consequently be weighed down and eventually turn into attachments. Of course, when appearances and dharmas are witnessed drifting with the whirling form–emptiness wheel, human compassion for life will intuitively arise. And since Buddhist compassion is above all a shadow of the self, it represents the open, beginner's state of mind of self-nature. It is self-unfolding and self-manifested, but it does not represent any value system, nor is it to be considered a kind of teaching or charity extended towards 'the other' by the subjective 'I'.

Compassion, being in itself anti-teaching, and anti-charity, is instead to be understood as an empathetic altruism of the mind whirling along with the form–emptiness wheel; it represents the greatest part of the Dharma, and the nobleness of human nature.

---

88 *Translator's Note:* 'Defilement' in Buddhism means impurities in the mind. Greed, hate and delusion are three typical defilements of Buddhist psychology.

The whirling emptiness of the form–emptiness wheel – with the Five Skandhas rotating along – can be understood as a metanarrative, which involves no value system, no imitation theory or reflection theory, but is a narrative about the primordial mind fulfilled jointly by language and the soul.

With its whirling, the form–emptiness wheel discards all conceptualised knowledge about the Five Skandhas, preserving only poetry. In this context, poetry refers to the primordial poetic state, which has so far remained untainted by the obstruction of poetic pursuit, and which alone testifies to the absence of meaning in the whirling of the form–emptiness wheel. This primordial poetic quality generated along with the whirling is the only true manifestation of poetry that is free from the bondage of poetry itself.

The Five Skandhas, as concepts, are dissolved once the form–emptiness wheel goes whirling; as a result, they display no distinction from each other as they rotate around emptiness. After all, the concept of Five Skandhas was created merely for expediency, and used only to be eventually discarded.

The Five Skandhas continually switch positions, as the form–emptiness wheel swirls along, and are eventually turned into emptiness. In fact, the swirling dissolves all skandhas into emptiness.

Through the whirling, reality gets dissolved, so is emptiness. The statement by Chan[89] master Zhaozhou 'the Buddha is

---

89 *Translator's Note:* Chan is the school of Chinese Buddhism, known as 'Zen' in Japanese.

vexation; vexation is the Buddha' is correct concerning the inter-relationship between the troubles of reality and the Buddha.

Through the whirling, all skandhas, like the Skandha of Form, become 'appreciable appearances' that are readily perceived by the senses without concealment or 'disturbance'. Each skandha is appreciable mainly to just one sensory system; for example, form is appreciable to vision, and mantra to hearing.

Emptiness serves as the motivating force for the whirling of the form–emptiness wheel (along with which poetry is generated). For example, when we see the appreciable appearance of 'form', we see it through 'emptiness'. Without 'emptiness', there is no 'form' to be seen. In other words, the very act of 'seeing' represents the manifestation of 'form'.

Emptiness is the cause, but not the essence; it is a crucial part of the whirling, but not a resolution.

Emptiness fuses together and becomes united with all the skandhas into 'one'. The Dharma is ultimately a monistic philosophy, and the form–emptiness wheel, through whirling, also gets dissolved into 'one'. 'One' in this context can be understood as a skandha that undergoes continual decomposition.

All metanarratives and meta-statements of the form–emptiness wheel stem from existence as well as from human perception of existence. During the process, emptiness serves as a bridge, or path, that connects the senses and their objects, and dissolves the gap between the two.

Meaning is absent from the whirling of the form–emptiness wheel, and 'one' is not a totality, but many individual, pure appearances that are devoid of meaning.

The form–emptiness wheel, along with its whirling, keeps dissolving itself, and keeps creating new form–emptiness wheels. The metaphorical 'one' is constantly dissolved into new 'ones' – there is no point in trying to make sense of what 'one' is, since there is no real 'one' in existence.

When the form–emptiness wheel first goes whirling, the universe emerges in its initial state, and all appearances are renewed as they were at first; the wheel continues rotating, keeping the primordial beginner's mind to its spiritual journey. This primordial state of mind is described in the following account in *Siddharta* by Hermann Hesse about the newly awakened Buddha, who appears rather like a non-academic phenomenologist:

> He looked around, as if he was seeing the world for the first time. Beautiful was the world, colourful was the world, strange and mysterious was the world! Here was blue, here was yellow, here was green, the sky and the river flowed, the forest and the mountains were rigid, all of it was beautiful, all of it was mysterious and magical, and in its midst was he, Siddhartha, the awakening one, on the path to himself. All of this, all this yellow and blue, river and forest, entered Siddhartha for the first time through the eyes, was no longer a spell of Mara, was

no longer the veil of Maya, was no longer a pointless and coincidental diversity of mere appearances, despicable to the deeply thinking Brahman, who scorns diversity, who seeks unity. Blue was blue, river was river... The purpose and the essential properties were not somewhere behind the things, they were in them, in everything.[90]

In my eyes, Hesse himself is also a skandha whirling with the form–emptiness wheel. Indeed, to the rest of the world, the Buddha, Hesse and I are nothing more than heaps of rhetoric or skandhas. We know nothing more than this about the rest of the world and each other.

To put it another way, we are all involved in the whirling of the language of skandhas. We all, the Buddha included, create our own Tathagata, and Tathagata creates all human beings and things.

In *Siddhartha*, Hesse announced through the Buddha: 'each one [of the stones] is Brahman'. Brahman is a Sanskrit word that refers to the highest universal principle, the ultimate reality underlying all phenomena. It stands for the realm of pure consciousness where the indestructible supreme spirit dwells, and where the form–emptiness wheel arrives from its whirling journey.

Tathagata, the enlightened Thus Come One of all appearances – he has already gone.

---

90 *Translator's Note:* Hermann Hesse, *Siddhartha*, ICON Group International, Inc, 2006, pp. 35–6

Winter Mountains (#8). *Shanshui* painting with poem in running script calligraphy (album leaf), ink on paper, 22.9 x 34.5 cm, by Dan Dang.

Winter Mountains (#8) (detail), by Dan Dang.

Chapter fifteen

Harmony within Skandhas of the Subjective Mind

The remaining four skandhas, namely, sensation *(vedana)*, perception *(sanjna)*, memory *(sanskara)*[91] and consciousness *(vijnana)*, define how the subjective mind works. Each functions in its own unique way, and together they work in harmony to substantiate the existence of the external world represented by the Skandha of Form. Like the team of four birds depicted in *Shi Jing*, who, with distinct forms and sounds, 'fly from the deep valley, move to the arbor, sing beautiful songs, only to seek response from friends'.[92]

The Chinese for sensation (*shou*) literally means 'receive' or 'accept', and the Skandha of Sensation functions by taking in information from the outside world through the sense organs. As Master Hongyi points out, 'the Skandha of Sensation refers to the mental process of taking in information from the external world, experiencing it, and then interpreting it – that is, judging whether the external stimuli brings pain or pleasure, or neither. It is, in a sense, closer to "emotion" than "feeling", for emotions are physical and cognitive responses to external stimuli, whereas feelings are mental associations and reactions to these emotions, shaped by individual temperament and experience, and belonging to the Skandha of Consciousness.'

---

91 *Translator's Note:* There have been various English translations for the Skandha of Memory including, for instance, 'mental conformation', 'impulse', 'volition', 'predisposition' and 'activity'. This book generally adopts Red Pine's translations for the Five Skandhas, but occasionally uses 'mental formation' to refer to the Skandha of Memory.

92 *Translator's Note: Shi Jing*, literally meaning 'The Classic of Poetry', is translated variously as the *Book of Songs* or *Book of Odes*. It is the earliest extant collection of Chinese poetry, comprising 305 works dating from the 11th to 7th centuries BC, and is one of the Five Classics, traditionally said to have been compiled by Confucius.

If the Skandha of Form represents the existence of an outside world, or the objective mind, the other four skandhas represent the existence of an inside world, or the subjective mind. Of course, this bipartite division of 'objective outside world' and 'subjective inside mind' eventually get united into one – 'emptiness'.

To put it another way, the Skandha of Form implies a looking outwards, though it should be noted that as human beings 'look', the physical world is 'looking' back. In contrast, the Skandha of Sensation implies a taking inward of both the objective outside world and the subjective inside mind.

The taking-in process of sensation occurs in two different ways: personal and non-personal. On the one hand, it is non-personal because the Buddha's exposition, though apparently based on the human perspective (of the physical being), transcends narrow personal experience. The Buddha, whose thinking–perceiving transcends dualities such as materialism versus idealism, is the orginal founder of Language Drift Theory. He is the one who sends the wheel of the skandhas adrift, whirling it around emptiness, to reach the level of living without walls of the mind, and so without fear.

On the other hand, the taking-in process of sensation is fulfilled in a personal way. Every individual sees the world and is influenced by it in a unique manner, forming strikingly varied illusions, even about the same thing. These illusions about things go adrift, develop into never-ceasing patterns, and may periodically meet different illusions about things. What has been taken into different individual minds can communicate with each other through the power of sensation, resulting in their drifting and, eventually, unity.

The Skandha of Form reveals what was previously obstructed and hidden, as in the case of the sky being revealed in blue or white. The Skandha of Sensation, by contrast, reveals illusions, namely, what are taken in and interpreted by the subjective mind. With help of sensation, the white and blue colour seen by the eyes is revealed as the sky; the roaring and splashing sound rushing into the ears is revealed as the sea. Just as joy and pain arise in succession deep within the heart, so such illusory phenomena arise one after another, as a result of the mind's taking in information from the external world.

People experience external events as objectively existing, and feel pain and joy. Such is the innate faculty of human beings. The Skandha of Sensation is the manifestation of this innate human faculty.

My *Gyeltang* series includes a poem titled 'Message'. It is my mind's 'experience' of 'a single bird':

> All of a sudden comes the message
> This morning, a large bird flew away to the east
> Its feathers slowly turn red
> Its body slowly turns blue
> Is it that bird, which flew away west at sunset yesterday
>
> That large bird's feathers slowly turn yellow
> Body slowly turns green
> This is the bird that took away the joy of growing up
>
> (Translated by Nick Rosenbaum)

Buddhist philosophy is a great poetic theory; at the same time, it provides a methodology for poetic studies. This methodology applies to Buddhist Chan (Zen) practice, too. The Five Skandhas represent five levels of poetic enquiry. Among these, sensation plays a key role in creating poetic feelings, since, like a door to the world, it takes in, interprets and reveals external illusory appearances, thereby enabling the unfolding and construction of the subjective mind. All through the process, the Chan (Zen) practitioner lingers at the door of sensation, seeking the right and unique path leading to his own mind.

Sensation is linked to form in that it is the passage for form to enter the mind. Therefore, sensation plays an indispensable part in discussing the other four skandhas.

The next skandha, the Skandha of Perception, according to Master Hongyi, refers to the mind's thinking process based on what sensation provides.

As I see it, perception is a follow-up to sensation. If sensation is where the external world drifts into the internal mind, perception is where the illusory appearances of the objective world are subjectified (positive, negative or neutral), re-created into appearances, and sent off for a new beginning. Perception is an important step for the mind to establish the existence of the external world.

Perception involves a thinking–perceiving process, but does not convey thoughts; it generates concepts, but is not the 'reactor' where concepts are conceptualised.

Perception takes place at the information taking-in level, where thinking–perceiving in the phenomenological sense is adrift. It is the stage where information obtained from form and sensation gets reshaped to produce language and symbols. So far as individual words are concerned, perception functions as the signifier, that is, the mental capacity conveying the sounds and images of words. It also takes the signified into scope, but does not go to the extent of identifying or specifying what is signified.

For instance, when you focus your camera on a spot on a wall for a close-up, you will find the spot to be a mysterious visual universe, which, in the inner mind's eyes, may resemble a melody or a piece of graffiti signifying the universe. The Russian painter and art theorist, Wassily Kandinsky, famously claimed that 'a spot is an abyss'. This spot, when taken as punctuation – say, a comma – is a simple sign in the language system indicating a pause or minute interval. Close up, however, the comma might look like a vast nebula.

To produce visual images means to focus in on what is attended to in the perceptual system. It implies a withdrawal from the world to set out on a journey of the mind into imagination.

For, different ways of looking at the same thing – from a macro perspective, metaphorical perspective, or micro perspective – will result in markedly different visions. None of the visions, however, represent the true original state of the world but are defined by emptiness.

To truly appreciate this world of forms, one needs a fresh perspective: thinking–perceiving. This requires a sensitive way of looking, and involves a looking out followed by taking in of information. With this out and in, thinking–perceiving is set awhirl and goes adrift.

The ways in which we observe the world reshuffle from moment to moment. The 'world' is a world created from structures adrift amid that reshuffling. The Skandha of Sensation is a phantasm layered upon a drifting world; the Skandha of Perception is yet another layer of phantasm.

The Skandha of Perception is a further coalescence of the world of form through cognitive activity. It also comprises the coalescence of thinking–perceiving.

Late one night, standing in the courtyard, I gazed up at the star-studded sky and became immersed in thinking–perceiving. This inspired the poem 'Courtyard':

> The deep depth of a word,
> bigger slightly than a real bird's nest
>
> I only want to set down a bit of
> suffering within my poems
>
> Take several sprigs
> Plant them in the threshold of my doorway
>
> At the foot of a tree I would
> Wait for a school of fish to swim here through
> the moonlight
>
> I want to study the language of those fish
>
> Study their imperturbable placidity within futility
>
> O fish, take me away
> Before the sincerity of the bright moon fades
>
> O fish, let me grow scales like moonlight
> Before the fading of nightscape
> Before I decode the rippled markings in the well
>
> (Translated by Nick Rosenbaum)

The *sanskara*-skandha, translated by Bill Porter as the Skandha of Memory, implies 'all the ways we have dealt with what we have experienced in the past and that are available to us as ways to deal with what we find in the present' (Bill Porter, p. 64). According to Master Hongyi, *sanskara* means 'make', or 'put together what has been received from the external world'. Chen Qiuping notes, '*sanskara* refers to the never-ending cycle of motion, driftage and volition-based actions'.[93] Master Guangchao also indicates, '*Sanskara* means "make", referring to responses of the mind to external environments, or to what has been perceived. Responses may occur solely within the mind realm – for example, the feeling of like or dislike on seeing a certain object.... The Buddha regards *sanskara* as just like other thoughts arising in the mind, and thus no different from sensation or perception. Whether the thoughts relate to greed, anger, kindness or evil...they involve the putting together of what the mind has received from the external world. But this is not controlled by the subjective mind – thoughts that arise in the mind may prove to be not what one wished for, and actions eventually taken may be not what one intended.'[94]

---

93 *Author's Note:* Lai Yonghai (ed.), *Chen Qiuping's Commentary on the Diamond Sutra and Heart Sutra*, Zhonghua Book Company, 2013, p. 126.

94 *Author's Note:* See Master Guangchao's 'Teaching Notes on the Heart of Prajnaparamita Sutra', from *A Variorum of the Heart Sutra*. Internal publication edited by Guanghua Temple in Putian, Fujian province, pp 89–90

As I see it, the Skandha of Memory means 'creation' or 'transformation'. When the millions of appearances go on the never-ending turning cycle, memory fragments are taken in (through sensation), coalesce (through perception), and are then sent adrift to a journey of transformation, or, re-creation. This re-creation process may occur internally, in the form of thoughts, or externally, in the form of actions (which produce karmic hindrances). Both thoughts and actions are in constant flux, though generally speaking, memory that is perceivable to the mind represents merely a certain provisional moment of memory (which is adrift), rather than memory that is capable of creation and transformation. The Skandha of Memory, from the Buddha's perspective, represents confusions caused by ignorance. In the end, memory refers to the creative activity of the mind, which, of course, is also a kind of emptiness, or one layer of emptiness.

The drifting and turning of memory transform the initial appearance (of the external world) into millions of appearances, and millions of appearances into the initial appearances. The provisional appearance of memory is like a halo whirling around the mind.

The Skandha of Memory is like a king of the mind, who, adrift in fear, is in constant need of self-salvation.

Self-salvation comes from transmuting all the events (mental appearances) of the world into 'poetic forms'. That is, to extend the skandhas of Form, Sensation, and Perception into millions upon millions of empty appearances expressed poetically. This creative activity of the universe is the requisite wave-flow of life's rhythmic cadence.

My collection *Early Spring* includes a poem entitled 'Small Stream for Small Fish', which reads as follows:

> At the dinner table, I eat
> The eternal patterns marked on small fish
> By day, the small stream of my homeland
> Swallows my mountain peaks
>
> At the dinner table, I eat
> The deathly silence into which small fish sink teeth
> By night, the riverbend of my homeland
> Sinks its teeth into my full moon
>
> (Translated by Nick Rosenbaum)

The most famous *gatha* of Master Huineng, sixth great patriarch of Chan (Zen) Buddhism, reads as follows:

> Bodhi originally has no tree,
> The mirror (like mind) has no stand.
> Buddha-nature (emptiness/oneness)
> is always clean and pure;
> Where is there room for dust (to alight)?
>
> (Translated by Yampolsky)

Another *gatha*, by eminent monk and master of meditation the Venerable Wenyi of the Five Dynasties period (905–60), also features beautiful poetic language.

> Those who don fine fabrics when sav'ring fragrant flow'rs
> Always shall their view of life differ so from others

Flecks of grey at hairlines today start their advance
Yet blossoms scarlet you see now,
last year's redness mirror

Like dew after morning fade such radiant colors
Sweet aromas drift off, tailing nightly zephyrs
Why then need we wait for with'ring on the vine
Only to, for the first time, their emptiness encounter?

(Translated by Nick Rosenbaum)

The Skandha of Consciousness, according to Master Hongyi, means 'distinguish' or 'identify the true essential nature of the external world created by the mind'. But, 'true essential nature' is something the Buddha disliked and even dispelled, for it is a dangerous concept, in which people, once swept in, often end up perpetually trapped. The *Abhidharma-kosha* ('Treasury of Abhidharma') points out that the heart, mind and consciousness are in fact variant names for one same thing, each signifying a different aspect of our mental activity. According to this text, 'heart is named to signify the arising of mental factors; mind to signify the thinking process; and consciousness to signify the function of discerning'. Hinayana teaches six types of primary consciousness (eye/visual consciousness, ear/auditory consciousness, nose/olfactory consciousness, tongue/gustatory consciousness, body/tactile consciousness, and mind/mental consciousness); meanwhile Mahayana further postulates a seventh (*manas*, or ego consciousness), and an eighth (*alaya-vijnana*, or seed consciousness). The Buddha asserts that existence has no permanent ontological nature. This is crucial to understanding 'the emptiness of dependent origination'.

The Skandha of Consciousness reveals the integrated mental process of becoming aware both of impressions from the five senses and of perceptions of mental objects, such as thoughts, ideas and emotions. It may occur either at the sensual or perceptual level, and is constantly shifting between the two, locally or globally. In one way, it brings about an overall transformation of the mind, with consciousness being activated or concealed at different places, then revealed and reactivated. Master Guangchao stated:

> Consciousness is the heart capable of sensation and perception about the external world – what eyes can see, what ears can hear, or what the mind thinks about. It has many layers. The first layer is the awareness of, or sensitivity to, the external world that it comes into contact with, which is yet to be named; this awareness is called consciousness. Based on this consciousness, the brain proceeds to the activities of discerning, evaluating, and analysing, which are in turn called perception, and mental formation (the Skandha of Memory). Some people, when awakened from their clinging, come to a sudden awareness of the existence of the 'self', but the Buddha tells us it is not the 'self' that exists, but 'the Skandha of Consciousness', which includes different types such as eye consciousness, ear consciousness, nose consciousness, tongue consciousness, etc.[95]

---

95 *Author's Note:* 'Teaching Notes on the Heart of Prajnaparamita Sutra' by Master Guangchao, *A Variorum of the Heart Sutra*, internal publication edited by Guanghua Temple, Putian, Fujian Province, p. 90

While often overlooked by Buddhist scholars, it should be noted that the first layer of consciousness mentioned here continues to be transformed into other layers of consciousnesses with various structures. What is clear and certain is that the Buddha saw no permanence in consciousness, nor did he set distinct boundaries for each skandha. To distinguish and discuss the skandhas is striving to do the impossible.

As I see it, however many layers of consciousness there are, the main point is the formation of certain concepts in the mind. The four skandhas of Sensation, Perception, Memory and Consciousness reveal a cycle of development, turning and drifting, first from the more preliminary sensual level to a more complex perceptual system, then back to the preliminary level. In this process, the Skandha of Form is swept in to become one link of the drift rotation. My observation is, of course, from the perspective of the history of human civilisation; it sends adrift not only the physical world, but also the world of knowledge and concepts. Rationalism, influenced by Plato, views the generation of concepts as the ultimate goal of knowledge. This, however, only represents the daydreaming and delusion of human beings. In fact, human civilisation history viewed from the perspective of the Dharma is no other than a history of day-dreaming to attain true Suchness.[96] It is doomed a futile effort, because, with the development of civilisation, human beings have

---

96 *Translator's Note*: True suchness (Sanskrit *bhūta-tathatā*, Mandarin *zhenru*), or 'thusness', is a word used in Buddhism to mean 'reality', or the way things really are. 'Suchness' is deliberately vague to keep us from conceptualising reality, whose true nature is ineffable, beyond description and conceptualisation.

gradually let go of existence based on a beginner's open state of mind, marked by perfect freedom, and set foot on a path towards the non-human. The Buddha gave no superiority to different layers of drifting skandhas. Each skandha attains its drifting and provisional existence at the moment when self-sufficiency and freedom is achieved.

The Skandha of Consciousness, as a form of perception, is on guard against the causal laws of rationalism. Buddhist teachings are innately opposed to the logocentrism of Western philosophy. In the eyes of the Buddha, consciousness is a knowledge model drawn backwards by the 'emptiness of dependent originations'. All layers of consciousness drift in emptiness. The arising of one dependent origination is immediately followed by the generation of another. 'Dependent origination' serves as the motivation of the turning or spinning activity, and gets dissolved through self-rotation. There is, therefore, no existence of causal laws in the logocentric sense.[97]

Ludwig Wittgenstein points out, '[W]hat is insidious about the causal approach is that it leads one to say, "Of course, that's how it has to happen". Whereas, one ought to say, "It may have happened like that, and in many other ways."'[98]

The later Wittgenstein, sharing the Buddha's thinking–perceiving, expressed outright opposition to logical deter-

---

[97] *Translator's Note*: Logocentrism is a philosophy holding that all forms of thought are based on an external point of reference which is held to exist and given a certain degree of authority.

[98] *Translator's Note*: Ludwig Wittgenstein, *Culture and Value*, revised edition, Wiley-Blackwell, 1998, p. 60.

minism. Viewed from the perspective of modern Western philosophy, both deserve to be called 'anti-philosophers'. The Buddha, as the pioneer of anti-philosophy, is the first ancestor of Language Drift Theory, which this book tries to elucidate. I, therefore, humbly call myself a follower of the Buddha, and of Wittgenstein.

In Chapter 10 of the *Diamond Sutra* the Buddha taught:

> Therefore, Subhuti, the Bodhisattva, Mahasattva, should thus produce a pure heart. He should produce that heart without dwelling in forms. He should produce that heart without dwelling in sounds, smells, tastes, tangible objects, or dharmas. He should produce that heart without dwelling anywhere.

That a bodhisattva should 'produce that heart without dwelling anywhere' serves as a core teaching for all Prajnaparamita sutras. Failing to grasp this teaching means a failure to approach the Dharma. In Chapter 18, the *Diamond Sutra* continues as follows:

> The Buddha told Subhati, 'all the various thoughts which occur to all the living beings in all those Buddhalands are completely known by the Tathagata. And why? All thoughts are spoken of by the Tathagata as no thoughts, therefore they are called thoughts. For what reason? Subhati, past thought cannot be got at, present thought cannot be got at, and future thought cannot be got at.'

As noted earlier, the four skandhas of the subjective mind are like a team of four birds with distinct forms and sounds that 'fly from the deep valley, move to the arbor, sing beautiful songs, only to seek response from friends'. But alas! If 'past thought cannot be got at, present thought cannot be got at, and future thought cannot be got at', what point is their 'seeking response from friends'?

The Buddha has disclosed the secret, so compassionately, yet so calmly and joyously, that I find myself having nothing to say.

All I can do is to belt out a song, while tears stream down my face.

Shanshui Ink Painting (#25). Album leaf, ink on paper, 17.5 x 23 cm, by Dan Dang.

Chapter sixteen

The Drifting and Turning of Skandhas

Every skandha is contained in other skandhas; every skandha contains other skandhas. No skandha exists by itself, or stays unchanged. Instead, all skandhas are constantly drifting towards each other and infiltrating each other. They exist only provisionally in a drifting state. To distinguish the Five Skandhas is a striving to do the impossible, because language is not able to give a full description of skandhas. Language can do no more than capture fragments of skandhas, which are but phantasms of provisional existence. There is no full picture of skandhas; if we must hypothesise one, it is the physical body. But this physical body is not real either, for the body-skandha is different for every individual body. Each body-skandha, adrift, exists momentarily in a state of constant flux, when it reveals itself in the form of a fragment of existence. The drifting of skandhas is as intriguing and elusive as that of sound and form.

We might understand the inner formation of the Five Skandhas by referring to the relationship between cloud and rain. According to a popular Chinese song, 'a piece of cloud, made from rain, is in the wind'. When the 'cloud' and 'rain', both manifestations of the Skandha of Form, come into view, they are captured by the mind only at the 'sensual' level, with yet no inner-connection with the viewer. Then they drift along in the mind realm to the 'perceptual' level, that is, to be perceived by the mind, so that when the song repeats 'oh, that piece of cloud made from rain', 'mental formation' comes into operation and metaphorical meaning unfolds in a mysterious way. Up to this point, no concept has been formed; it only occurs in the melancholic line 'in the wind the cloud drifts, broken-hearted; in every tiny droplet your image is reflected', when what has been perceived in the mind is recognised, evaluated, and emerges as 'consciousness'. It is at this moment that the concept of 'love' is generated. Likewise, when we judge someone to be loving and loyal, the judgement is made based on his previous behaviour patterns, or in other words, the impression of him in our memory works to form the concept of 'love and loyalty'. When the singer sings: 'in every tiny droplet your image is reflected', the metaphor of rain (droplet) symbolising tears successfully creates a concept that is both melancholy and beautiful.

Concepts are expressed through ideas. The same idea in the same context presented in the same manner, through drifting to any the different layers outlined above, may emerge as a skandha of different types. Sometimes it reaches only the preliminary layer of 'form', and at other times it may reach the layer of 'consciousness', producing metaphorical concepts.

Viewed from the perspective of *mano*-consciousness (*manas* or ego consciousness, the seventh layer), the millions of things in nature are nothing but emptiness. Can you move a mountain into your mind? No. What is moved is the image of the mountain, rather than the mountain itself. Can you make a river flow into your heart? No. What your heart feels is only the visual image or burbling sound of the river, even if you are physically swimming, fish-like, in the river. Therefore, the relationship between humanity and nature is marked by emptiness; what is real in nature is not likely to be captured by the human mind other than some fragments. The same is true for romantic relationships. However much you are in love with someone, it is not possible to capture all the physical skandhas of that person. All you can access are limited skandhas that emerge at particular moments, or that are manifested through outward behaviour. In other words, what his/her inner mind is processing is never fully revealed. Of course, your own being is also only partly revealed to others through the accessible elements of the skandhas (personality factors). Loving feeling, as a kind of imagining, represents the various skandhas coalesced and going adrift. No one knows where this path of imagination leads; nor is its dream-like drifting accessible to the mind. Though your loved one is with you in the physical sense, his/her spiritual being may remain somewhere beyond your reach. This can cause distress, which, in turn, leads to various kinds of clinging or attachment.

The person you love, as a coalescence of skandhas, is in constant flux, and thus cannot be defined as existing in any fixed place. He/she may be next to you physically, but you do not know where his/her skandhas or spiritual self is drifting. Physical being and spiritual being, phantasm and reality, are all but delusions. Delusion is inescapable suffering for all humans, which can be transcended only through the teaching of emptiness. It is undeniable and inescapable that human beings exist like a distorted phantasm, an image in the mirror. Both the physical existence and mental existence of humans are but transitory, dream-like phenomena. Nevertheless, it is on the basis of this complexity of human existence that the beauty of literary and artistic creation is made possible. The unfolding of existence is, in itself, a skandha with unsurpassed beauty, marked by the actions of aggregating, dispersing, or intervals between the two.

There are times when the 'self' is a *mano*-consciousness (ego-consciousness). To exist means to be aware of the self; existence is manifest in the helplessness of the self. This might not be how the Buddha in an enlightened state sees things. Even the Buddha, however, does not always exist in emptiness, adrift, but is afflicted, from time to time, by the ego-consciousness (*mano*-consciousness) and the seed consciousness (*alaya-vijnana*). This is because the Buddha, despite having surpassed sentient existence, and attained truth and freedom, is not a divine being; instead, he is of this world, and is essentially no different from other sentient beings.

Why do we like to watch films, when we are aware that what happens in a film has nothing to do with our own life? As the plot develops, we become increasingly involved, and with it experience emotional highs and lows. We willingly allow ourselves, almost compulsively, to be swept away from reality into the film. There is no obvious connection between the reality around us and the absurd phantasms on the screen, but our hearts and minds are drawn to the film because it is in tune with the created, illusory world of the mind. So, it is not the film that is absurd, but the fact that we are hallucinated by it. My book *Absurd and Intriguing Games* ostensibly discusses and comments on literary works, but it is really talking about human beings. For the life of humans is an absurd and intriguing game, a dream or bubble in which millions of physical skandhas turn and tumble.

Therefore, the Five Skandhas, in my view, represent the greatest poetic theory in history.

Art at the highest level is created free from the bondage of any value system.

If an artist works with a certain particular value system in mind, his work seeks to serve the values it embodies, for instance, by creating certain standards for virtues, or for characters exemplifying such virtues. There is nothing wrong with this. In fact, most Chinese literary works throughout history have followed the tradition of 'literature for conveying the Dao (Tao)', with 'literature' taken as a tool serving the purpose of conveying the Dao.

Nevertheless, in the eyes of the Buddha, 'literature for conveying the Dao' is nothing but a phantasm, revealing human beings' clinging to the self. Let me venture to ask you, artists, are you working in the service of one concept, or for a multitude of concepts? Are you aware how your mind gets swept away and concealed by concepts? Or, have you willingly surrendered your mind to be concealed and swept into the abyss of concepts? After all – as I know –'clinging to the self' in itself is intriguing enough to most artists. Art turns out to be the greatest source of attachment. This fact, unfortunately, may not be revealed to us unless we see with insights granted by Prajnaparamita.

Though each of the Five Skandhas reveals a different path we might take in our search for reality, they remain a virtually interconnected and interdependent whole, represented as the skandha of emptiness. Being 'empty of self-existence', they stand for five ways of approaching emptiness, like five petals of the prajna-flower. Coming together, form, sensation, perception, memory, and consciousness return to the unity of emptiness; moving apart, they drift and whirl around emptiness. In contrast to Christianity, which posits a personified God as the ultimate reality, Buddhist philosophy sets the teaching of 'emptiness' as its cornerstone. True emptiness produces marvellous existence (existence of non-existence); and marvellous existence is in never-ceasing whirling and drifting.

Buddhist philosophy is distinct from the religion of Buddhism. In the framework of Buddhist philosophy, both the Buddha and the Buddhadharma are empty; they hold all sentient beings to be equal and seek to lead all beings to enlightenment. But in the framework of Buddhism as a religion, the Buddha becomes a personified divine being, offering to ferry sentient beings to enlightenment in a condescending manner. As a holistic entity created by Buddhist philosophy, emptiness can be viewed as a concept, or a non-concept defined by emptiness. In this context, emptiness, or skandha of emptiness, functions as a verb instead of a noun.

Hence, the concept of form–emptiness, created by combining emptiness and form, dissolves the assumption that there exists a holistic material world. This happens at the very moment form–emptiness starts to move as a verb and goes adrift. In other words, the drifting of the Five Skandhas serves as a driving force in dissolving this assumed 'holistic material world'.

Various philosophic theories obtain provisional existence through creation of different concepts; they are then dissolved at the moment this provisional existence goes adrift. For instance, phenomenology temporarily exists in form; reception aesthetics temporarily exists in sensation; value-based literature temporarily exists in perception and consciousness. The Five Skandhas whirl around emptiness, producing the essence of Language Drift Theory.

Lesser artists create by following artistic concepts; greater artists create in clinging to the poetic self; the greatest artists create by countering traditional poetry in the generation of a fresh poetic spirit.

The recording of history and writing of literature are both essentially poetic. What language conveys, however, is not intrinsic reality but an interpretation of reality. For, no historical reality per se exists in any language system; what does exist is the intrinsic reality of language itself, manifested in the revolving and drifting of language-based skandhas. In this sense, the Five Skandhas can be considered a language system, whirling and adrift, comprised of form, sensation, perception, memory and consciousness.

Master Hongyi exemplified the revolving and drifting activity of the Five Skandhas in the following cycle:

Forms in the external world produce various sensations.

Sensation produces various perceptions.

Perception produces various mental formations.

Mental formations influence consciousness in the mind.

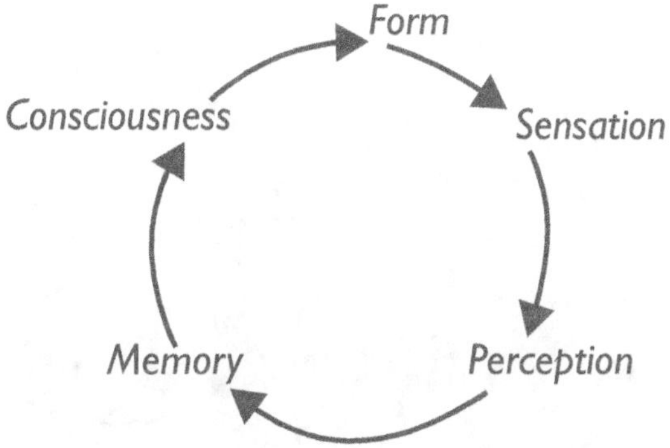

Consciousness in the mind produces forms in the external world.

Figure 1: Diagram showing the endless cycle of birth and death

I hold a slightly different view from that of Master Hongyi, believing that the Five Skandhas do not revolve or drift in a single direction. Rather, the drift activity is bi-directional or even multi-directional. Every skandha on the cycle can function as the starting point of the rotation; the same skandha can also function as the end point, which marks the unfolding and provisional existence of appearances. Further, every skandha may contain other skandhas; every skandha is a united whole with all five skandhas temporarily present; it can be a phenomenon adrift, a fragment of the external world, or a fragment of the internal consciousness. This view of the relationship between the skandhas and their activities can be shown as follows:

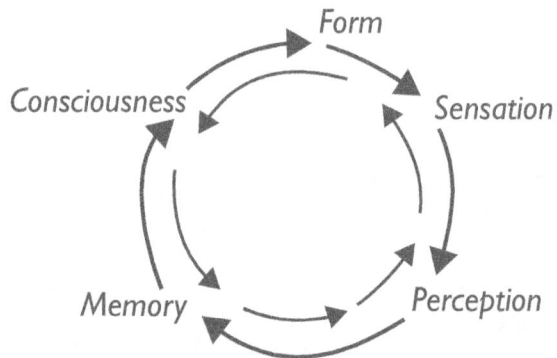

Figure 2: Diagram showing the bi-directional movements of the Five Skandhas

The song 'Alive' by Sa Dingding, with lyrics written by the contemporary song-writer Gao Xiaosong, expresses the provisional moment in which the aggregates cycle and rotate, going adrift:

> Once upon a time the winter was cold, ah
> The summer saw rain, ah, water
> In autumn carried from afar
> Your warm voice, ah, warm
>
> You said back then behind the house
> Was bright white white white snow, ah
> In a mountain canyon's wind
> A yellow banner flutters, ah
>
> I see a mountain eagle flying
> above two lonely fish
> Those two fish traverse a river
> Waters salty lik the sea

That riverwater cascades down
To meet people as they break
People walk along, their bodies covered
With dust shed by mountain eagles

(Translated by Nick Rosenbaum)

All things are alive; they are seen, sensed, or perceived, and eventually they disappear. The cycle of life and death is a manifestation of inconstancy, which is the intrinsic reality of the mental or spiritual world. Inconstancy marks the constant reality of existence in the spiritual, linguistic, cultural and poetic sense. Indeed, reality itself is empty; emptiness is not constant. Master Hongyi explained inconstancy in this way:

> If form is real, it should be constant and unchangeable; but in fact, the Skandha of Form in the external world is constantly in flux. Thus, mountains, rivers, and lands suffer grand changes. Even 'I' myself am constantly in flux – 'I' turn into a different 'self' every other year, every other month, and every other day. In fact, the 'self' becomes different with every other breath, for, one breath is taken and my body has undergone numerous changes. Most typically, the blood in my body changes position and quality and performs different functions when I breathe in or out. Further, such changes occur not only in a breath; they occur in every fraction of a second. Since all things are in such constant flux, they are empty of any intrinsic existence.[99]

---

99 *Author's Note*: From *Li Shutong's Exposition of Buddhist Sutras*, Shaanxi Normal University Press, 2008.

Awareness that the Five Skandhas are in constant rotation may cause people of sensitive mind to find themselves losing the sense of something permanent. Therefore, an enlightened being must be one who makes possible a journey afar by drawing support from fragments of imagination. A person in the spiritual sense is inherently a 'wanderer', though, of course, 'somewhere afar' in this context is again an imagined place, albeit one that plays a vital role in the journey to the Other Shore to achieve self-salvation.

Shanshui Ink Painting (#27). **Album leaf, ink on paper, 17.5 x 23 cm, by Dan Dang.**

Chapter seventeen

Skandhas Adrift under Provisional Names

The Buddhadharma is a method for generating poetry. Poetry employs relative, provisional language, causing drift. The skandha of the Buddhadharma, and of poetry, likewise employs such relative, provisional language, with words following one after the other, like wave after wave.

In poetry, provisional language is in itself ultimate truth and transcendent wisdom (prajna). Using provisional language to cultivate the heart is an impossible task, which we nevertheless undertake, and that undertaking forms the sorrowful song of life. All great poetic expression that has its origin in our lives is without exception a mix of joy and sorrow.

I have a poem dedicated to a young muse, entitled 'Big Dipper':

> To taste the sour ache in Sister Muse's silver key
> A high mountain curls up, fermenting beneath starglow
> To its side, coils a long river
> Ever so meek and mild
>
> To taste the azure strewn by Sister Muse into the wide ocean
> Peaks on peaks at sunrise ceaselessly roar
> Covered in splatters of blood
>
> (Translated by Nick Rosenbaum)

'Provisional language' bears some similarity to 'nominal existence'. According to *Commentaries on the Three Treatises* by Ji Zang[100], 'dependent originations, being nominal existence

---

[100] *Translator's Note:* Ji Zang (549-623) was a great Dharma master in the Madhyamika tradition. He first propagated the teachings of *The Three Treatises* (*Sanlun*) in China with his famous commentaries. *The Three Treatises* are the three principal Madhyamaka texts composed

by nature, are understood as conventional truth. Nominal existence cannot signify permanent existence; nor can it signify permanent non-existence.'

From the perspective of the Buddhadharma, all appearances, including the physical body, are provisional language, or, provisional names. Shariputra, the early disciple of the Buddha, for instance, is a provisional name signifying the noumenon made of the constantly changing and drifting Five Skandhas. Of course, the so-called 'noumenon' itself is merely an appearance in provisional existence.

The noumenon of Buddhadharma is a coalescence of all dharmas. Since 'all dharmas are defined by emptiness', the noumena of all dharmas, marked by the flux of the Five Skandhas, are also empty. Reality, or the true appearance of things, might be taken as the opposite of 'emptiness', but in the thinking–perceiving system of the *Heart Sutra*, reality is also emptiness.

The Five Skandhas certainly concern 'reality'; without reality, they would make no sense. But 'reality' is introduced here for the teaching of 'emptiness'. 'Form', being part of reality, reveals the state of existence of matter and events, as well as that of our physical body. With the help of the sensory and perceptual systems, we are able to know, feel and understand thousands of things in the world, by perceiving how they exist. But the *Heart Sutra*, contradicting common sense, explicitly declares that 'all dharmas are defined by emptiness'. This confuses many readers. But, in

---

by Nagarjuna and Aryadeva, which were translated into Chinese by Buddhist monk Kumarajiva in the early 5th century.

fact, in teaching about the emptiness of all dharmas, the Buddha assumes the existence of a 'reality' in the mind. This is a crucial step, showing that the Buddha has gone beyond the duality of 'materialism' versus 'idealism'. Nevertheless, rather than existing as something (whether as nature, life or the body) with an intrinsic self, this 'reality' exists only in the form of a language system, a physical body, a concept, or a certain perspective. This view reveals the truth about how the skandhas exist in the mind – the truth of existence as manifested in the language system.

The thinking–perceiving of the Buddhadharma has an eternal 'contemporariness'. It aims at solving such big questions as attachment to non-concepts and creation of non-culture, a goal similar to the great ambition of Wittgenstein. Alain Badiou points out:

> The fact that Wittgenstein's ontological construction somehow operates in a tight to-and-fro movement between 'what is' and 'what is said' is appropriate for the goal he sets himself: the valorisation, against the restricted space of scientific propositions, of the mystical element, which manifests itself but cannot be said. There is no doubt a specular relationship between the theses on being and the theses on the proposition. This link is contained in the notion of the picture, which is introduced axiomatically: 'We picture facts to ourselves' (2.1). These pictures are on the order of language. But in the final instance it is that which is not in the picture that is 'higher', having an authentic value. The point of being that is 'truest' is not captured in

the specular relationship in which the ontology of the world and of language is constructed. It is obtained there where 'something', which is precisely not a thing, comes up as a remainder of this relationship.

This idea of the 'remainder' can be found in every anti-philosophy, which certainly builds very subtle networks of relations but only to track down the incompleteness in them and to expose the remainder to its seizure by way of the act. This is precisely where anti-philosophy deposes philosophy: by showing what its theoretical pretension has missed and which in the end is nothing less than the real. Thus, for Nietzsche, life is that which appears as a remainder of every protocol of evaluation. Just as, for Pascal, Grace is entirely subtracted from the order of reasons; for Rousseau, the voice of conscience from the preaching of the Enlightenment; for Kierkegaard, existence from the Hegelian synthesis. And for Lacan, we are familiar with the theme of jouissance and the Thing to which it is yoked, which the philosopher cannot and does not want to know.[101]

The 'ontological construction', in this context, is simply a linguistic tool, not a noumenon in the world. It is, therefore, none other than another 'provisional name'.

The question is, how does 'reality' turn 'empty', or, in other words, how do different forms turn into emptiness? The answer is – through provisional language. Drifting

---

101 *Translator's Note:* Alain Badiou, *Wittgenstein's Antiphilosophy*, Verso, 2011, pp: 93–5.

between 'what is' and 'what is said', provisional language makes expression possible and easy to fulfil. It remains in the cycle of drifting, joining with 'what is' and 'what is said' to generate meaning, create mystical poetry, and produce the mind. During this process, linguistic features are either semantically sharpened or shattered. Again, according to Alain Badiou:

> The didactic destination of philosophy joins a syntax that is always tempted by mathematics to a semantics that is always tempted by hermetic poetry. It aspires in one and the same movement to crystalline univocity and to absolute equivocation.[102]

This shows the instinctive efforts of linguistic expressions to approach reality. 'Provisional language', as a linguistic expression, manages to break through the dilemma of 'univocity' and 'equivocation'.

Reality is not to be turned into emptiness without assuming provisional names. For example, the philosophy of Plato would not have existed if he had not hypothesised the Idea, that is, 'the Really Real'.[103] Though he never said it, what he called 'Idea', in my view, is also an assumed provisional name, as shown in *The Republic*.

---

102 *Translator's Note*: Alain Badiou, *Wittgenstein's Antiphilosophy*, Verso, 2011, p. 165

103 *Translator's Note*: For Plato, the real world is a place of Ideas, which he names 'the Realm of the Forms'. These Forms are called 'the Really Real'. The world of the Forms is rational and unchanging; the world of physical appearances is changeable and irrational, and is only real to the extent that it succeeds in imitating the Forms.

It is worth noting that the drifting and revolving of the Five Skandhas involves provisional names for the true appearance not only of the Skandha of Form, but also of the other four skandhas. Through employing provisional names, the mind, as a coalescence of skandhas, goes into the cycle of drift and transformation, instead of falling into deadening stagnation. In a way, the various skandhas drifting and revolving in the mind are a sign of life.

But in what way do provisional names exist and how do they make possible the transformation of true appearances into emptiness? The Buddha teaches that 'all dependent originations are defined by emptiness', implying that all things and events in the world, including the drifting of the Five Skandhas, exist in the chain of causation in our sensory and perceptual systems. To be more exact, skandhas are dependent origination manifested. Dependent originations may exist as reality, or as emptiness; both, however, turn into provisional names once coming into the chain of causation. Therefore, the chain of dependent originations is the chain of provisional names, unfolding the action of the mind. This is not what the Buddha said directly in his teaching, but is surely implied in his thinking–perceiving system.

It is also worth noting that skandhas may dependently arise out of some sort of certainty at a local level, or out of pure chance, for there is neither permanent certainty nor contingency in the sense of determinism. That 'dependent arising is empty of inherent existence' should not be taken as any type of determinism.

Skandhas are dependent arising with no set origin; dependent arising is skandhas in marvellous existence.

Judged from the perspective of rationality in Western philosophy, the Buddhadharma presents no such concept as truth, standing for some unchanging knowledge. In the Buddhist view, any 'unchanging knowledge' could be a source of attachment. Attachments represent the defilement and sickness of life, and are not able to go adrift. Everything is dependent for its existence on something else; everything arises in a way that is dependent on particular conditions, and ceases to be with the cessation of those conditions. That is the pattern of life as well as of the physical body. Once this is clear, the emptiness of all dharmas refers to the lack of any permanent, unchanging true appearance; there exist in the mind only provisional names, or the skandha of provisional names.

It is a mistake to understand 'emptiness' as absolute 'nothingness', for emptiness does not mean that nothing exists. Rather, it means that there is an absence of intrinsic nature in the temporary dwelling of skandhas in their aggregation and dispersion. 'Emptiness' in this context, therefore, is to be understood as a verb, and 'temporary dwelling' marks marvellous existence. Both 'emptiness' and 'temporary dwelling' are provisional names. Becoming aware of this brings about a mixed feeling of joy and sorrow, which is characteristic of the awakening process. 'Temporary dwelling' is like the glittering of light in the process of dependent origination; it occurs as an outcome of some causal conditions, and ceases when those conditions change or disappear. Such is the joy as well as the sorrow of life.

As conditioned dharmas, life, in the spiritual sense, is no other than heaps of 'dreams, illusions, bubbles, shadows', which, nevertheless, are not marked by nihility. While many people assume Buddhist teachings to be pessimistic, I view them as great 'joyful thoughts' concerning the existence of life. Once awakened to the law of dependent arising, one will experience spiritual bliss, as if being caressed on the cheeks by a warm and gentle spring breeze, in which a million acres of fragrant orchids joyfully flicker and sway. The Buddhadharma provides a solution to the problem of spiritual existence by breaking down clinging and attachments, bringing life back to peaceful stillness. It represents true compassion and love of life.

After the line of the *Heart Sutra* '...all dharmas are defined by emptiness', the next continues 'not birth or destruction, purity or defilement, completeness or deficiency'. This alludes to the 'empty' nature of provisional names. In the perpetual changing process of skandhas governed by the law of dependent arising, there is no true existence of either 'birth' or 'destruction'. Rather, resorting to provisional language helps transcend the duality of birth and destruction (which describes the state of existence), of purity and defilement (which signifies value judgement and concerns), and of completeness and deficiency (which tells of changes in quantity or degree). All, however, concern the emptiness of provisional language.

Certainly, the arising and cessation of the skandha of provisional language, like that of clouds, carries internal forces. But overall, it exists in an equilibrium of forces, like the supposedly heavy clouds, which, though containing tons of water, succeed in floating in the 'empty' sky; or the Earth, which, while revolving around the sun, reaches equilibrium with the sun. When a being is in a state of equilibrium, it will not be aware of its own weight. For example, a healthy person is normally not aware of his or her own body weight, while a sick person experiences difficulty in moving his/her body. Equilibrium of forces is the self-nature of beings, and adopting provisional language makes it possible to express this self-nature, though linguistic expression itself is a kind of drifting away from the true self.

That 'all things are empty' marks an awakening to the self-nature. It begs the following questions. If there is a self-nature of existents, why are they defined as being 'empty'? And if there is no such self-nature, how do existents exist as 'all things'? Self-nature is the original way of existence of all things, but it is not the essential nature. Even if the essential nature does exist, there is nothing we can do but keep silent, for we understand the world by way of provisional language, whereas the silent, vague 'essence of the world' is beyond linguistic expression. Human beings discussing the so-called 'essence of the world' is like roundworms living in a person's intestines, discussing the existence of their host. Even if roundworms could indeed carry out the discussion, all they can do would be to assume the concept of a 'host' without being able to see the host. It is a similar case with humans living in nature – it is ridiculous and meaningless to discuss the 'whole' or essence based on hypothesised concepts.

The Buddhadharma is on constant guard against humans turning to the 'non-human', which is exactly where its greatness is manifest.

The Buddhadharma opposes the Buddhadharma. To unfold the self-nature of things which exist in a state of non-essentialness marks an awakening to the principle of 'dharma being anti-dharma', and to the pure thinking–perceiving for the first time. Appearances are distinct in terms of self-nature, and this distinction marks the fundamental difference between them. It creates a difference as large as that between human beings and pigs, despite the two share a high percentage of genetic similarities.

Differences in self-nature lie not simply on the level of names and appearances. Self-nature is a kind of conditioned arising.

The self-nature of things, by producing a limitless number of provisional names, generates a variety of skandhas in different forms for the mind to perceive.

At the moment when 'joyful thoughts' arise, provisional language, adrift, also arises or ceases to be.

The skandha of the Buddhadharma, and of poetry, likewise employs such provisional language, with words following one after the other, like wave after wave.

Winter Mountains (#10). *Shanshui* painting with poem in running script calligraphy (album leaf), ink on paper, 22.9 x 34.5 cm, by Dan Dang.

Winter Mountains (#10) (detail), by Dan Dang.

Chapter eighteen

An Unobstructed Mind

The *Heart Sutra* can be seen as the 'skandha of the heart-mind'. The emptiness of all thoughts in the mind generates a poetic marvellous existence.

The ideas of the Buddhadharma are a poetics unsurpassed over all time; the Buddhist sutras represent fascicle upon fascicle of epic poems for the spirit. The misty quality of the poems, like a dream, a fantasy, bubbles or shadows, lies in the assumption inherent in each one that a mind exists, or innumerable minds. The poetry is generated in such a mind and then passes through all minds, observing all minds.

My poem 'Spring Waters' reads:

> Spring waters gurgle
> A commotion in the granary
> Scraping the granary empty
>
> Grinding waters whisper
> A lamentation in open pastures
> Pushing up tiled houses as they flow
>
> Stones and water are eternally locked in contest
> Cool down? Or gush ahead?
>
> Why
> Do stones pile up to the clouds
> Towering thousands of leagues high
>
> Why
> Does spring water rock thousands upon thousands of boats?
> Thousand and thousands of empty caverns

(Translated by Nick Rosenbaum)

The mind is inherently empty. Every person exists in the 'emptiness' of his mind. When skandhas traverse in emptiness, poetry and specific minds are generated.

The mind is inherently empty. Millions of thoughts travel and drift in emptiness. We usually assume the existence of a person's mind after ascertaining the person exists. And sometimes, the existence of a person is based on assumptions, as is the case with Descartes when he states, 'I think; therefore I am.'

But when we talk of a person, that person exists only in an abstract sense as a concept. That is how everyone exists in other people's eyes. To assume the existence of a person's mind is to embue that mind with something meaningful, that is skandhas. A mind into which some type of skandha drifts instantly becomes unique and specific; a mind in which skandhas go adrift becomes an accessible mind; a person with an accessible mind becomes a tangible person. This is the starting point of existing as a person, though the point may be either trusted, assumed, or put in doubt.

Any person who is alive has a mind to assume or to trust, where countless drifting skandhas are constantly generated.

Loneliness often results from doubting the possibility of accessing a mind, or from uncertainty about the truthfulness of a mind. A common question asked is: 'Is that what you truly think?' Because it is indeed difficult to ascertain the truthfulness of a mind.

Therefore, people try all manner of means – theories, logical reasoning, deduction, and so on – to prove the existence of a truthful mind. Ask yourself, when you declare, 'She loves me', are you genuinely sure of what you say? Or does there remain, in fact, some room for doubt? I venture to say that most of the time the latter is the case, because it is difficult to predict the drifting pattern of skandhas. The sentence, 'You are my love', may have a totally different meaning when followed by different punctuation marks – a full stop, a question mark, or an exclamation mark – each signalling a different path to understanding the mind. For the mind to be perceived, skandhas, in the form of moral standards or other evaluation criteria for discernment, must first be brought in. For example, skandhas attached to a man's declaration, 'I love her', probably include such evaluations as: she is pure, she is kind, or she is diligent. Since each skandha reveals only one aspect of a person's mind, it is very difficult to gain a full understanding of the mind.

There are infinitely many paths to a person's mind. Different people take different paths by bringing in different skandhas.

Though skandhas brought to the mind may not be true, their linguistic expressions can hold truth. When the two are united into one, based on shared truth, skandhas will be revealed in pure truth. Such pure skandhas do not necessarily represent any tangible, physical materials; they may represent some imagined truth. Scottish poet Robert Burns, known as 'the ploughman poet', wrote, 'My heart is in the Highlands. My heart is not here. My heart is in the Highlands, a-chasing the deer.' How can his heart be in the Highlands, if it is not one of the imagination?

Whether or not Burns' heart is true, depends, therefore, on whether or not we believe in the pure skandhas in his heart.

The act of believing drives the pure skandhas adrift. To believe means to put faith in something. The conviction, 'I love her', as a skandha, does not stand unless on the foundation of faith.

Occasionally, to have faith in a heart, or a mind, is to believe in a dream, and to deem true a whole new world.

The Six Roots – eye, ear, nose, tongue, body and mind – provide six pathways for skandhas. The corresponding Six Dusts – shape, sound, smell, taste, feeling and thought – represent six modes for the manifestation of skandhas. And the Six Consciousnesses – eye-consciousness, ear-consciousness, nose-consciousness, tongue-consciousness, body-consciousness and mind-consciousness – represent various types of creation by skandhas. The Six Roots, Six Dusts and Six Consciousnesses together comprise the Eighteen Spheres, which represent eighteen domains where skandhas, adrift, work to establish experiences of the world. Each domain retains its unique functions and characteristics, while being permeated by and mixed with skandhas from other domains, so that skandhas from different domains coexist in an interdependent way. Typical examples include the skandhas of 'storm' and 'flag', 'sea' and 'sailing', and 'fleet' and 'lighthouse'.

The Six Roots, as 'default settings' for human beings, make it possible for people to experience and exist in the physical world. Such existence, however, is not the same as intrinsic nature. In fact, people are unaware of the intrinsic nature of the world, since they are but a type of conditioned phenomenon, a dependent arising categorised as 'human'. The Six Dusts refer to six kinds of information collected through the sense organs, which, as drifting phantasms like dust, because of their defilement, are major hindrances to enlightenment. The Six Consciousnesses are distinction-making activities of the mind, which enable people to perceive the way the world exists, and to distinguish different categories of skandhas, which, again, are but phantasms. The Eighteen Spheres reveal eighteen different patterns in which skandhas aggregate, each being one way to unfold existence. Out of these eighteen patterns are produced countless further skandhas, which, through drifting, return to the eighteen patterns.

Thousands and thousands of skandhas invite me to fly, but, unfortunately, I remain trapped in where I am. This is my destiny as a human being.

The Eighteen Spheres aggregate into one mind or numerous minds. Skandhas drift within every individual mind, like clouds transforming into various patterns. The mind itself is a form of skandha; it transforms into numerous skandhas. Skandhas drift within and beyond skandhas.

The *Diamond Sutra* states that the Bodhisattva 'should produce that heart without dwelling anywhere'. *Vimalakirti Sutra* also states, 'all dharmas are established on the fundamental [basis] of non-abiding'. Both imply that the existence of the heart/mind, whatever forms it may take, should be based on assumptions, rather than on something static and permanent, for no mind is static and permanent.

The full title of the *Diamond Sutra* is the *Diamond-Cutting Prajnaparamita Sutra*, with 'diamond' used as a metaphor implying that the sutra is hard and sharp, can cut through any obstacles and bring one to the Other Shore of enlightenment. At the same time, a diamond is shining and beautiful, just like the noblest, brightest and completely unobstructed mind of the Buddha.

Mind, dharmas, and skandhas exist in oneness. When they unite into one, heroic spirit and romantic feelings blossom into a fragrant orchid flower in my mind.

Given that the existence of mind, dharmas, and skandhas is located in a place of 'non-dwelling' and 'non-abiding', so all skandhas are 'non-existent' from the perspective of Language Drift Theory. Non-existence is the true nature of 'non-dwelling' and 'non-abiding'. The *Heart Sutra*, demonstrating unprecedented firmness, removes multiple obstructions of attachment with the following grand declarations centring around 'non-existence':

> in emptiness there is no form, no sensation, no perception, no memory and no consciousness;
> no eye, no ear, no nose, no tongue, no body and no mind;
> no shape, no sound, no smell, no taste, no feeling and no thought;
> no element of perception, from eye to conceptual consciousness;
> no causal link, from ignorance to old age and death,
> and no end of causal link, from ignorance to old age and death;
> no suffering, no source, no relief, no path;
> no knowledge, no attainment and no non-attainment;
> for nothing is to be attained.

'Non-existence' not only removes the Six Roots, Six Dusts, Six Consciousnesses and Eighteen Spheres, but also rejects the Twelve Links of Dependent Arising, Four Noble Truths and all other concepts and skandhas. Only the boundless realm of 'non-existence' is left. All this is presented so impressively one cannot help but jump up and cry out in amazement.

Of course, 'non-existence' does not equal nothingness. Non-existence, as a concept, is to be understood as a verb; and the verbal form 'being non-existent' is a synonym for 'emptiness'. When we assume the existence of a mind, we assume the existence of 'emptiness' as a skandha or a provisional name. In fact, all are provisional names – mind, dharma, skandha, appearance, emptiness and non-existence. Provisional names exist in provisional names; they coexist and interdepend on each other.

In all linguistic activity, provisional names are the only true reality, just as emptiness is the initiator of the rhythm patterns of great music.

Bill Porter records:

> When Hui-k'o asked Bodhidharma to help him make his mind stop, the First Patriarch of Zen said, 'Show me this mind of yours, and I'll make it stop.' Hui-k'o answered, 'But I've looked everywhere, and I can't find the mind.' Bodhidharma said, 'There. I've stopped it for you.' Thus, in the light of emptiness, we say that the eyes and the other powers do not

exist, which does not mean that we have no eyes, only that the eyes are not ultimately real, just a convenient fiction to which we give a name.

(Red Pine, p.102)

Though defined by emptiness, the mind has sensory as well as perceptual abilities. These abilities manifest the power of vitality, and vitality needs provisional language to get expressed and verified, for vitality is empty of self-essence, and cannot go adrift without help of the latter. The 'drifting', or being adrift, of skandhas such as the mind, dharma, non-existence, emptiness, etc., is the true reality of existence; and existence in the sense of 'temporary dwelling' requires the presence of concepts (that is, provisional names). But the purpose of employing provisional names is not to keep them but to eventually drop them.

Wittgenstein points out:

> My propositions serve as elucidations in the following way: anyone who understands me eventually recognises them as nonsensical, when he has used them – as steps – to climb up beyond them. (He must, so to speak, throw away the ladder after he has climbed up it.)
>
> He must transcend these propositions, and then he will see the world aright.
>
> (T6.54) (Wittgenstein, p.89)

A line in a popular Chinese song goes, 'My true heart / I present to you, this loneliness / I keep to myself.' 'True heart' and 'loneliness' are two bridges of skandhas, and singing is an act to remove the bridges.

The following lines from Cao Cao's 'A Short Song' best tell how I feel:

> Bright is the moon in the sky,
>   when can I ever embrace it?
> Sorrow is born inside the heart,
>   it can never be brought to an end.[104]

(Translated by Wu Shengfu and Graham Hartill)

Being emotionally attached to a loved one can be a beautiful experience, and the wretch suffering from it certainly knows how this emotional attachment inspires poetry.

---

[104] *Translator's Note*: Cao Cao, courtesy name (*zi*) Mengde, was a Chinese warlord, statesman and poet of the end of the Han period (206 BC–AD 220).

Shanshui Painting with Figures (#1). Album leaf, ink on gold-flecked paper, 50.8 x 33.2 cm, by Dan Dang.

Chapter nineteen

The Twelve Links of Dependent

Arising, the Four Noble Truths and 'That Person'

In my *Gyeltang* series of poems, there is one called 'That Person':

That person
    comes from the rolling boil of a leopard's eye
    the swaying burden on a pack animal's back

That person
    makes treestump watch over treestump on
    the high plateau
    rattan entwine with rattan

That person
    leaves a space in the fence for cattle and goats
    two door bars, smooth and round

That person
    readies a path for the bright sun
    stones from the saddle between mountains

That person
    readies a pivot point for the dark night
    the bitter regret of a sky full of stars

That person
    is planted in cow dung by the spring breeze to rear again
    for wormwood to grow over their head

(Translated by Nick Rosenbaum)

It doesn't matter who 'that person' is. What matters is to realise that every person can be 'that person'. Every person is on the turning wheel of dependent arising, as a physical being instead of a conceptual one. Meanwhile, concepts, merged with specific skandhas, help make the abstract existence of humanity conceivable, explainable and accessible. The Twelve Links of Dependent Arising, the Four Noble Truths and other similar concepts are all created for this purpose. When the Buddhadharma gets 'trapped' (expressed) in language, these concepts are used cautiously, and then discarded in the activation of counter-concepts. In the words of the *Diamond Sutra*, 'the Buddhadharma is not the Buddhadharma'.

'That person' could be the Buddha, or me, or a flower, or a shining crescent moon.

'That person' is the form of all phenomena in the world, and the appearance of love and compassion; it is the assurance of love and the dismissal of hate.

The Twelve Links of Dependent Arising and the Four Noble Truths combine to build one domain after another in the heart of 'that person'.

The Twelve Links of Dependent Arising are ignorance; volitional action (*kamma*); conditioned consciousness; name and form; the six senses; sense impressions; feelings; craving; attachment; becoming; birth; and old age and death.

According to the *Vinaya Piṭaka* (*Basket of Discipline*, Yuanheng Temple Edition), which is the Buddhist canon recording the Buddha's rules of discipline for monks and nuns:

> On
> [1] ignorance depends
> [2] *kamma*; on *kamma* depends
> [3] consciousness; on consciousness depends

[4] name and form; on name and form depends
[5] the sense organs; on the sense organs depends
[6] contact; on contact depends
[7] sensation; on sensation depends
[8] desire; on desire depends
[9] attachment; on attachment depends
[10] existence; on existence depends
[11] birth; on birth depends
[12] *dukkha*; old age and death, sorrow, lamentation, misery, grief and despair.

Commentators on the *Heart Sutra*, including, for example, Master Hongyi, mainly hold that 'ignorance' and 'volitional actions', as actions taken in the past, are causes, whereas 'conditioned consciousness', 'name and form', 'the six senses', 'sense impressions' and 'feelings' are results experienced in the present. Meanwhile, 'craving', 'attachment' and 'becoming', as actions taken in the present, are causes, whereas 'birth' and 'old age and death' are results to be experienced in the future. This describes the causal link of dependent arising in the Buddhist system, which may or may not be relevant to 'that person'.

Sutra expositors see time as linear, represented by the past, present and future. From the perspective of the Buddhadharma (not religious Buddhism), however, the unceasing movement of dependent arising does not drift in a linear chronological order. The Twelve Links are twelve kinds of skandha, each of which may serve as a starting point (where skandhas come into being) or end point (where skandhas cease to be) of dependent arising.

The Four Noble Truths are suffering, source, relief and path. Like the Twelve Links of Dependent Arising, they represent doors or thresholds through which people who 'take actions' can walk in or out – that is, enter the world (beginning of dependent arising) or leave the world (cessation or end). Master Hongyi points out that the first noble truth teaches that life is suffering resulting from *samsara*; the second noble truth teaches that craving and fundamental ignorance are the cause of suffering; the third teaches that putting an end to craving brings about enlightenment; the fourth teaches that there is a path to free us from suffering. The first two truths (suffering and source) describe the state of existence in the world; the other two truths (relief and path) illustrate the cessation of existence in leaving the world. Master Hongyi continues to elucidate, 'Practitioners of Prajnaparamita find all dharmas (those of this world or not of this world) empty. Hence "no suffering, no source, no relief and no path".'

Like the Twelve Links, each of the Four Noble Truths, as first taught by the Buddha to his followers, can be viewed as both a starting point (where skandhas come into being) and an end point (where skandhas cease to be) of dependent arising.

The Twelve Links of Dependent Arising and the Four Noble Truths are both conditioned and conditioning links on the wheel of life of 'that person'. The explanation of the pattern of dependent arising seems to suggest that human beings are trapped in its endless moving chain, but this is not what the Buddha wishes for. In a sense, the *Heart Sutra* and the *Diamond Sutra* provide a kind of reflection on both the employment of linguistic means to express the inexpressible and the construction of the chain of the Twelve Links.

Therefore, caution should be taken in carrying out any cause–effect chain analysis. Of course, elaborations on the Buddhadharma have always been restrained and cautious, revealing the purest and most compassionate concern for the worldly existence of sentient beings. While the Buddhist analysis of the links of dependent arising is highly logical, the greatness of the Buddhadharma lies rather in its anti-logic and anti-conceptual nature. That explains why, although concepts like the Twelve Links and the Four Noble Truths had to be created for the sake of elaborating on the Buddhadharma, they are eventually dismissed and discarded in practising the Buddhadharma.

And that is why the *Heart Sutra* states:

> no causal link, from ignorance to old age and death,
> and no end of causal link, from ignorance to
> old age and death;
> no suffering, no source, no relief, no path;
> no knowledge, no attainment and no non-attainment;
> for nothing is to be attained.

The implication is that, since everything is part of an endless web of interconnections and undergoes a continual process of transformation, a skandha (which might be a concept) has already completed its life cycle at the moment it first arises. Both dependent arising and cessation are defined by emptiness. Consequently, though marvellous existence keeps arising in the mind of 'that person', it is all by its nature empty.

The spring winds blow over the earth, bringing the land back to life and preparing for a new cycle of birth and death. Sadly, 'that person' is nowhere to be found. But the Buddha, leading us down the path seeking 'that person', transforms failure into joy. This might serve as a point of understanding the last words of Master Hongyi: 'Joy and sorrow are intertwined.'[105]

I too have been constantly searching for 'that person', as instructed by the Buddha.

Ultimately, the cyclical motion of the Twelve Links and Four Noble Truths represents the movement of the mind, that is, the rotation of skandhas or appearances manifesting the spiritual existence of beings. Things and beings perpetually arise and cease because other things and beings perpetually arise and cease. Although a cause–effect relationship is involved in this process, it is not fixed. A cause that exists right now may within a minute become an effect, and vice versa. Moreover, there is no first cause. Beings and phenomena brought into existence by other beings and phenomena create further beings and phenomena. Sometimes, cause and effect provide different elaborations on the same skandha, such that from one perspective it is a cause, from another an effect.

---

105 *Translator's Note:* Master Hongyi is known to have written his last calligraphy:, 'Joy and sorrow are Intertwined' (悲欣交集), three days before he passed away.

The chain of dependent causation is comprised of intriguing fragments of skandhas.

Spiritual existence is comprised of a series of skandhas and fragments of skandhas that are adrift. Nothing is absolute, for no beings or phenomena exist independently of other beings and phenomena. Life is random, for everything is but fragments of skandhas in temporary dwelling.

And the existence of 'that person' is also random. Once a certain condition exists, a temporary cause–effect relationship is established. But there is no first cause, or, if there is, it is also adrift. Therefore, cause and effect itself is empty – after all, the Buddhadharma sees the self-nature of all beings and phenomena as empty.

'That person' is an empty appearance where skandhas dependently arise and drift about.

One cause and effect disappear at any moment, and be transformed into another cause and effect. Like the constant light–dark changes in our vision, cause–effect links undergo constant changes.

When conditions are appropriate and the Twelve Links arise, a cause–effect chain is established, but then another condition arises, causing the cessation of the previous chain and bringing into being of a new one. This is how all phenomena in the world arise, exist and are extinguished.

Just as a cause–effect chain temporarily arises, so 'that person' comes into being and has a transient existence in the world.

The cause–effect chain is sent on the path of going adrift at the random moment the right condition arises. Such paths appear or disappear with the emerging or vanishing of conditioned causes. The Twelve Links may be viewed as twelve doors or paths leading to potential chains of dependent arising, but this does not mean that cause–effect chains are pre-determined. Rather, the Twelve Links and Four Noble Truths are merely tools for the elaboration of the Buddhadharma. Like all linguistic expressions, they serve merely as examples illustrating how the chain of cause and effect operates in the potential cycles of life. To show the full picture goes beyond the capacity of language. Or rather, there exists no cause–effect chain that fully illustrates the patterns of existence either within or outside the world. The Buddhadharma teaches no personal transcendent God of creation, and this is where Buddhist philosophy differs strikingly from Christian theology.

Though dependent origination is itself emptiness (as was declared by Nagarjuna), this dependence is not necessarily empty from the perspective of the spiritual existence of human beings, but may become a cycle of real appearances. Once humanity chooses to 'believe' in the existence of emptiness, emptiness turns into reality. That is to say, there exists a dependent cause–effect chain between emptiness and reality. In the eyes of the Buddha, there is neither absolute reality, nor absolute emptiness; there are only skandhas in an endless cycle of dependent arising.

Reality and emptiness co-exist; they are essentially one, each an aspect of the other. 'That person' is both empty and real, since it is both generated from the self and dissolved within the self.

Indeed, 'that person' has come into the world. The Twelve Links are the turning of the provisional existence of 'that person' and the paths created after the emergence of a certain skandha. Thus, the shift of the links on the chain of dependent arising does not follow any fixed pattern, but is incidental and unpredictable.

Incidental, changeable and impermanent – these are words that correctly describe the way 'that person' exists. And the concept of 'impermanence' sets apart the Twelve Links of Dependent Arising from modern deductive reasoning.

Karen Armstrong says:

> The terms used in the Chain are rather obscure. 'Name and form', for example, was simply a Pali idiom for a 'person'; 'consciousness' (*vinnana*) is not the totality of a person's thoughts and feelings, but a sort of ethereal substance, the last idea or impulse of a dying human being, which has been conditioned by all the *kamma* of his or her life.
>
> (p. 160)

And:

> There are no fixed entities in the Chain. Each link depends upon another and leads directly to something else. It is a perfect expression of the 'becoming', which the Buddha saw as an inescapable fact of human life. We are always trying to become something different, striving for a new mode of

being, and indeed cannot remain in one state for long. Each *sankhara* gives place to the next; each state is simply the prelude to another. Nothing in life can, therefore, be regarded as stable. A person should be regarded as a process, not an unchangeable entity. When a *bhikkhu* meditated on the Chain and saw it yogically, becoming mindful of the way each thought and sensation rose and fell away, he acquired a 'direct knowledge' of the Truth that nothing could be relied upon, that everything was impermanent (*anicca*), and would be inspired to redouble his efforts to extricate himself from this endless Chain of cause and effect.

(p. 162)

That 'a person should be regarded as a process', means to see him or her as the coursing and drifting of all the kinds of skandhas that incidentally arise in life. This is the destiny not only of 'that person' or me, but also of the Buddha, who has seeped into my heart.

'That person' leaps millions of years, coalescing into the real and true skandhas of a person. 'That person' comes into our lives to swim you and me to the Other Shore. 'That person 'sees' or 'is seen by' the shifting and turning of poetry, unbroken across the continuum of thought after thought. 'That person' harmonises with the rhythm of the Five Skandhas, the Twelve Links of Dependent Arising and the Four Noble Truths, and harmonises with the arrival, precisely on time, of thousands of reams of written mantras, their poetry revealed in the expanse of space and time. 'That person' casts off the fetters of grasping for an ego, achieving the freedom of action that is harmony of body and mind.

I have a poem to recite entitled 'A Thousand Years Later', which guides me out of this endless, myriad-fold cosmos where all thoughts pour without ceasing through the mind:

> A thousand years later
> Shoots of rice grow to the tips of mountains,
> stones rest on jade
> You, Sister Muse, remain anchored
> In a dream where time slips through fingers
>
> And I, too, am in my homeland
> Joining the plough ox to guzzle at a long river
> Clamorous the light cast off rippling water
> Cascading wave after wave
> Breaking apart cups for wine
>
> For a thousand years
> I chased after your pendants of light, sister
> Hung all throughout this drunken heart
>
> For a thousand years
> I sat astride a saddlehorse, nostrils aheave
> Galloping out of the forest
>
> For a thousand years
> I locked up falcons of iron
> So I might be released
> To fly over sky and land
>
> (Translated by Nick Rosenbaum)

Winter Mountains (#11). *Shanshui* painting with poem in running script calligraphy (album leaf), ink on paper, 22.9 × 34.5 cm, by Dan Dang.

Winter Mountains (#11) (detail), by Dan Dang.

Chapter twenty

Nirvana and the Mantra Flow

The Sanskrit word *nirvana* literally means the 'quenching' or 'blowing out' of a flame. Only later was the word used to refer to a state of total liberation in which the mind awakens from all delusions. This state is marked by liberation from bondage, cleansing of defilements, cessation of suffering, and, eventually, obtaining freedom from the cycle of rebirth and re-death.

The Mahayana School of Buddhism stresses the ultimate enlightenment of all beings, and thus recommends that those who have attained nirvana remain in the world to assist others who have not yet reached it. Therefore, the Buddha in Mahayana is the Buddha of this world, and bodhisattvas in Mahayana are bodhisattvas of this world. Bill Porter indicates:

> Nirvana is simply the final delusion. Thus, Mahayana sutras never tire of telling us that bodhisattvas do not attain nirvana and even avoid it, that their goal is elsewhere, namely the liberation of all beings. This is also the view of the *Perfection of Wisdom in Twenty-five Thousand Lines,* which states that while bodhisattvas lead others to nirvana, nirvana itself is a dream or delusion. And, in Chapter Two of the *Lotus Sutra,* the Buddha tells Shariputra and the other arhans seeking to become bodhisattvas that the nirvana they have attained is really but an imaginary oasis on the road to buddhahood.
>
> (p.138)

That nirvana is 'but an imaginary oasis on the road to buddhahood' reveals a significant aspect of the Buddha's thinking–perceiving system. It clarifies that nirvana is a state reached in the process of practising Buddhism, rather than an ultimate destination. From the perspective of Language Drift Theory, nirvana is to be viewed as a verb connoting the drifting and coursing of skandhas along the path to buddhahood. 'Oasis' in this context refers to the domain where nirvana, as a skandha, provisionally dwells. Like beauty that exists for beauty's sake, this domain also serves as its own purpose; it does not have origination, nor will it come to pass. It is a domain shining with beauty, similar to that of a splendid rainbow after rain, or the glorious glow of sunset. As a beautiful domain for provisional existence that also 'spills over' itself in constant flux, nirvana represents the state reached through spiritual practice, and the true way in which humanity is supposed to exist.

Therefore, reaching nirvana is a return to one's true self-nature. In some ways this evokes Tao Yuanming's celebration of his retreat to his home village in the poem 'Ah, homeward bound I go!':

Ah, homeward bound I go!

Why not go home,
seeing that my field and garden with weeds are overgrown?
Myself have made my soul serf to my body:
why have vain regrets and mourn alone?

Fret not over bygones and the forward journey take.
Only a short distance have I gone astray,

and I know today I am right,
if yesterday was a complete mistake.

Lightly floats and drifts the boat,
and gently flows and flaps my gown.
I enquire the road of a wayfarer,
and sulk at the dimness of the dawn.[106]

(Translated by Lin Yutang)

The *Heart Sutra* states, 'Therefore, Shariputra, without attainment, bodhisattavas take refuge in Prajnaparamita and live without walls of the mind. Without walls of the mind and thus without fears, they see through delusions and finally nirvana.' By 'seeing through' delusions, the mind makes its way back to its original pure and true nature, which was a feature of the state of human existence in the beginning, but later became increasingly 'defiled' as humanity grew increasingly attached to the world. The domain where the skandha of true self-nature exists is a realm of total purity, where non-existence exists provisionally. It is an imaginary oasis for emptiness. The *Diamond Sutra* expounds on how to develop a pure heart as follows:

> Therefore, Subhati, the Bodhisattva, Mahàsattva, should thus produce a pure heart. He should produce that heart without dwelling in forms. He should produce that heart without dwelling in sounds, smells, tastes, tangible objects, or dharmas.

---

106 *Translator's Note:* The poem was written by Tao Yuanming (365–427), also known as Tao Qian, a Chinese poet of the Six Dynasties period. The English translation is by writer Lin Yutang (1895-1976).

He should produce that heart without dwelling anywhere.[107]

People may reach nirvana in an unlimited number of ways. Anything can serve as a path to nirvana; it may be a warm teardrop, a fragrant plant, a piece of fruit, or a road. Those things sung in the mind, all reside in the fertile oasis of the nirvana-skandha; it is like the self tasting delicacies. One poem from *Shi Jing* describes a joy of this kind:

> We gather and gather the plantains;
> Come gather them anyhow.
> Yes, gather and gather the plantains,
> And here we have got them now.
>
> We gather and gather the plantains;
> Now off the ears we must tear.
> Yes, gather and gather the plantains,
> And now the seeds are laid bare.
>
> We gather and gather the plantains,
> The seeds in our skirts are placed.
> Yes, gather and gather the plantains,
> Ho! safe in the girdled waist.[108]
>
> (Translated by James Legge)

---

107 *Translator's Note:* Hsüan Hua, *Diamond Sutra: A General Explanation of the Vajra Prajna Paramita Sutra,* Buddhist Text Translation Society. 1974, p. 123

108 *Translator's Note:* The translation is from: *The Book of Poetry,* translated by James Legge, Shanghai, The Chinese Book Company, 1931.

Therefore, as I see it, nirvana is a verb. Only when we pass through poetry, where the spirit of people and of things come together, do we achieve the fruition of nirvana, and does the practitioner's heart find nourishment.

Some say that Chan (Zen) is a flower. I say, nirvana is a flower. The Buddha stood before his disciples, held up a flower and smiled, thereby substantiating a fragrance within the heart that is inexpressible in words. The Buddha was a great poet. There was a fullness of poetry that emanated naturally and freely in his mind — that poetry is the Buddha himself.

As I see it, nirvana is not the cessation of birth and death. It is the blossoming of poetry written in the flesh. In the moment of our lives when we write poetry, through the gateway of non-dualism that is the poetic blossoming between things and the self — that is the gateway to nirvana.

I have a poem entitled 'Trumpet Flower Sweet as Clove' (referring to the Chinese name for the morning glory, which is shaped like the horn of a trumpet). This poem writes of the skandha of nirvana, and the gateway of non-duality between things and the self):

> Trumpet flower sweet as clove
> Slowly grows cold under setting sun
> Also growing cold is the spot where
> A crane sits on the water buffalo's spine
>
> Sister Muse, your agate
> Is red as the branding irons of heaven

Trumpet notes sweet as clove
Slowly fade into the distance under setting sun
Also fading into the distance is the aged tail
A dustwhisk trailing the water buffalo's spine

Sister Muse, your song
Is like the round moon climbing a staircase to heaven

(Translated by Nick Rosenbaum)

'Sister Muse' is a flower. She is my oasis of nirvana.

To summon Sister Muse, one needs to employ figurative language and let it flow like the flow of a chanted mantra. The three thousand waters of the Ruo River,[109] or ten thousand books of poetry and prose, are all manifestations of the flow of chanted mantras. All events, phenomena and objects, all sweet-smelling flowers, are there to assist practitioners in their spiritual seeking, till they finally reach nirvana. In the oasis of nirvana, emptiness is reality, and reality is emptiness; flowers are fair, and the moon beautiful, but they are manifestations of the nirvana-mind in the imaginary domain of language.

Sister Muse is a flower. She is my oasis of fragrance. In the domain of my mind, she transforms into a flow of the fragrance-skandha, sending unexpected emotions adrift, along with the skandhas of sounds and forms.

---

109 *Translator's Note:* In Chinese, 'three thousand waters of the Ruo River' is often followed by 'I will only take one scoop'. This is a well-known declaration of love which means although there is an abundance of water, I will only take one scoop, that is choose just one among thousands.

The skandha of mind aggregates into the flow of chanted mantra, like the convergence of wave into wave.

The sound and form of Sister Muse in the oasis of fragrance is like the flow of a chanted mantra.

The flow of a chanted mantra represents the height of linguistic expression. The *Heart Sutra* chants in such a way that it flows unobstructed:

> All buddhas past, present and future
> also take refuge in Prajnaparamita
> and realise unexcelled, perfect enlightenment.
> You should therefore know the great mantra of
>   Prajnaparamita, the mantra of great magic,
> the unexcelled mantra,
> the mantra equal to the unequalled,
> which heals all suffering and is true, not false,
>
> the mantra in Prajnaparamita spoken thus:
> 'Gate gate, paragate, parasangate, bodhi svaha'.

This mantra reveals the prajna that was once kept secret. Constant chanting of it will lead one to reach the realm of freedom, and to live without walls of the mind.

Mantras are a mystical form of invocation. They do not have a specific meaning, but that is precisely what makes them meaningful. The author of the *Heart Sutra* first ushers in the reader with a statement that seems to have a clear meaning: 'The noble Avalokiteshvara Bodhisattva, while practising the deep practice of Prajnaparamita, looked upon the Five Skandhas and seeing they were empty of self-existence....'

He ultimately brings the journey to an end, however, with a mantra-like flow that seems meaningless. This resembles the life journey of human beings, which may start with the creation of meaning, but ends with drifting in non-meaning.

A great literary text is similarly a mantra-like flow, both revealing absurdity that 'is true, not false', and unfolding meaning and non-meaning along with its drifting and coursing.

The *Heart Sutra* may be regarded as revealing the existence of just one individual, namely, the Buddha; or it can be seen as referring to any enlightened being – for instance, Sister Muse and myself. One needs to believe in what is identified as 'true' and 'not false', for believing gives birth to marvellous existence, and to you and me.

And that is where the secret lies: unless you believe in mantras and their powers, they will not affect your life. When you do believe, they lead the skandha of mind to break free from attachments, and break down the walls of mind.

Thus, the point of mantras is not their semantics, but to call out, or to summon. Bill Porter states:

> A mantra is like a magic lamp. If you rub it correctly, its resident genie will appear. During Hsuan-tsang's stay in India (630-644), he once traveled through Andhra Pradesh and came to a cavern where the monk Bhavaviveka lived during the previous century and where he was said to have chanted a mantra every day for three years in order to invoke the appearance of Avalokiteshvara. The resident genie

of this mantra, however, is not Avalokiteshvara, but Prajnaparamita, the Goddess of Transcendent Wisdom and the Mother of All Buddhas, and it turns out she is already present. Thus, bodhisattvas who know this mantra know their mother.

(p. 153)

The summons is the flower blooming to a hidden rhythm. The opening of that rhythm is the flow of a chanted mantra.

Summoning all buddhas throughout space and time is the prajna mother of buddhas – Prajnaparamita, the Perfection of Wisdom. This is the skandha of the heart's 'scattering of seeds'.

I have an ode entitled 'Scattering Seeds on the Mountain':

> Afternoon.
> Ploughshare bends wood
> Scattering seeds with you, sister
> Silvery bean sprouts amidst scattered showers
> Pile like snow on mountain top
>
> Sunset.
> Hillsides crumble
> As wooden plough casts shadows
> Empty hollow of the cowbell
> Summons a pair of bamboo baskets
> Yoked to shouldered pole

Twilight.
Butterflies stave off spring flowers
As they bend towards temple drums at dusk

Go home.
The gleaming clarion high in the clouds
Brims over with wine

(Translated by Nick Rosenbaum)
August 12, 2016, at Yanlu

Winter Mountains (#14). Shanshui painting with poem in running script calligraphy (album leaf), ink on paper, 22.9 x 34.5 cm, by Dan Dang.

Winter Mountains (#16). *Shanshui* painting with poem in running script calligraphy (album leaf), ink on paper, 22.9 x 34.5 cm, by Dan Dang.

The Prajnaparamita Heart Sutra in Sanskrit

(Transliteration)

prajnaparamita hridaya sutran

arya avalokiteshvaro bodhisattvo
gambhiran prajna-paramita caryan caramano
vyaavalokayati sma panca skandhas
tansh ca svabhava shunyan pashyati sma
iha shariputra
rupan shunyata shunyataiva rupan
rupan na prithak shunyata shunyataya na prithag rupan
yad rupan sa shunyata ya shunyata tad rupan
evam eva vedana sanjna sanskara vijnanam
iha shariputra sarva dharmah shunyata lakshana
anutpanna aniruddha amala avimala anuna aparipurnah
tasmac shariputra shunyatayan na rupan
na vedana na sanjna na sanskarah na vijnanam
na cakshuh shrotra ghrana jihva kaya manansi
na rupa shabda gandha rasa sprashtavya dharmah
na cakshur-dhatur yavan na manovijnanan-dhatuh
na avidya na avidya kshayo
yavan na jaramaranan na jaramarana kshayo
na duhkha samudaya nirodha marga
na jnanan na praptir na-apraptih
tasmac shariputra apraptitvad

bodhisattvo prajnaparamitam ashritya
viharaty acitta-avaranah
citta-avarana nastitvad atrasto
viparyasa atikranto nishtha nirvanah
tryadhva vyavasthitah sarva-buddhah
prajnaparamitam ashritya
anuttaran samyak sambodhim abhisambuddhah
tasmaj jnatavyan prajnaparamita maha-mantro
maha-vidya mantro
anuttara mantro
asama-sama mantrah
sarva-duhkha prashamanah satyam amithyatvat
prajnaparamitayam ukto mantrah tadyatha
gate gate paragate parasangate bodhi svaha

The Prajnaparamita Heart Sutra in Chinese

(Xuanzang translation)

玄奘译《般若波罗蜜多心经》

观自在菩萨，行深般若波罗蜜多时，照见五蕴皆空，度一切苦厄。舍利子，色不异空，空不异色，色即是空，空即是色，受想行识，亦复如是。舍利子，是诸法空相，不生不灭，不垢不净，不增不减。是故空中无色，无受想行识，无眼耳鼻舌身意，无色声香味触法，无眼界，乃至无意识界。无无明，亦无无明尽，乃至无老死，亦无老死尽。无苦集灭道，无智亦无得，以无所得故。菩提萨埵，依般若波罗蜜多故，心无挂碍，无挂碍故，无有恐怖，远离颠倒梦想，究竟涅槃。三世诸佛，依般若波罗蜜多故，得阿耨多罗三藐三菩提。故知般若波罗蜜多，是大神咒，是大明咒，是无上咒，是无等等咒，能除一切苦，真实不虚。故说般若波罗蜜多咒，即说咒曰：揭谛揭谛，波罗揭谛，波罗僧揭谛，菩提萨婆诃。

The Prajnaparamita Heart Sutra in English

(based on Red Pine translation)

The noble Avalokiteshvara Bodhisattva,
while practising the deep practice of Prajnaparamita,
looked upon the Five Skandhas
and seeing they were empty of self-existence,
5   said, 'Here, Shariputra,
form is emptiness, emptiness is form;
emptiness is not separate from form,
form is not separate from emptiness;
whatever is form is emptiness,
whatever is emptiness is form.
The same holds for sensation and perception,
memory and consciousness.
10   Here, Shariputra, all dharmas are defined by emptiness,
not birth or destruction,
    purity or defilement, completeness or deficiency.
Therefore, Shariputra, in emptiness there is no form,
no sensation, no perception, no memory and
no consciousness;
no eye, no ear, no nose, no tongue, no body and no mind;

15   no shape, no sound, no smell, no taste,
no feeling and no thought;
no element of perception,
from eye to conceptual consciousness;
no causal link, from ignorance to old age and death,
and no end of causal link,
from ignorance to old age and death;
no suffering, no source, no relief, no path;
20   no knowledge, no attainment and no non-attainment;
for nothing is to be attained. [110]
Therefore, bodhisattvas take refuge in Prajnaparamita
and live without walls of the mind.
Without walls of the mind and thus without fears,
25   they see through delusions and finally nirvana.
All buddhas past, present and future
also take refuge in Prajnaparamita
and realise unexcelled, perfect enlightenment.
You should therefore know the great mantra of Prajnaparamita,
30   the mantra of great magic,
the unexcelled mantra,
the mantra equal to the unequalled,
which heals all suffering and is true, not false,
the mantra in Prajnaparamita spoken thus:

35   *'Gate gate, paragate, parasangate, bodhi svaha.'*

---

110 *Translator's Note:* As noted in Chapter One, the author believes that punctuating after this line makes better sense, though previous versions of the *Heart Sutra* have traditionally punctuated before this line. For example, Red Pine's version goes as: '... and no non-attainment. Therefore, Shariputra, without attainment, bodhisattvas take refuge in Prajnaparamita, ...'.

Notes on The Prajnaparamita Heart Sutra

Title

prajna 般若

The Sanskrit word *prajna,* or English prajna, is often rendered as 'wisdom', though some scholars propose 'beginner's mind' (*chuxin* in Chinese, meaning the open state of mind of a beginner). In fact, prajna is not to be understood as a noun with a fixed meaning, but a verb whose meaning is adrift. In other words, prajna refers to a state of growth, from before the generation of knowledge, to the moment knowledge is generated. We can see prajna as a process whereby wisdom, or *chuxin*, is first generated and then goes adrift. It represents the motion of life which, as an energy driving the mind into movement, undergoes endless cycles of driftage among and around the three planes of prajna: prajna of the world, prajna free of the world, and prajna of transcendence. Therefore, prajna should not be regarded as a static concept, but as a path, or a process of drifting.

paramita 波萝蜜多

This Sanskrit term literally means 'perfection' or 'accomplished', but is often translated as 'reaching the Other Shore', implying the practices through which human beings succeed in escaping this 'shore' of delusion and reaching enlightenment. Therefore, *paramita* is also spiritual liberation, a path or process along which the mind and meaning drifts.

heart 心

The original Sanskrit term *hridaya*, literally means 'core' or 'essence', and was traditionally translated into Chinese as *xin* ('heart'). Great Chan (Zen) Master Zibo points out that the word 'heart' is used figuratively to imply that this sutra contains in its few lines the essence, or the condensed meaning, of the whole of Prajnaparamita ('perfection of wisdom'). Just as prajna and *paramita* are to be understood as kinds of activity or movement of the mind rather than static concepts, so 'heart' should not be regarded as a fixed concept. It is to be seen instead as the field in which wisdom is first born, a channel for forces to connect. Like the terms prajna and *paramita*, the word 'heart' remains in a continuous state of drift.

sutra 经

The Sanskrit word *sutra* literally means 'thread' or 'string', in a reference to the physical format of the Buddhist scriptures, which were traditionally threaded together. It is typically used of oral teachings thought to have come directly from the Buddha, or expositions of the Buddha's teaching by his disciples.

Line 1
Avalokiteshvara 观自在

Master Xuanzang translates the name Avalokiteshvara into Chinese as Guanzizai. *Guan* means 'look upon', 'observe', or 'contemplate'; *zizai* describes the joyous state of being spiritually free and unfettered. Before Xuanzang, Kumarajiva translated the name as Guanshiyin, with *shiyin* meaning the 'cries of the world' that are being observed. A simplified variant, Guanyin, means 'observing cries'. Xuanzang and Kumarajiva translated the name based on 'arya avalokiteshvara', which is a variant of 'avalokiteshvara' in Sanskrit. The Chinese simplified variant 'Guan-yin' literally matches 'avalokiteshvara'.

Avalokiteshvara (Guanzizai) is one of the most revered bodhisattvas of the Buddhist pantheon. The bodhisattva's chief attribute is compassion, a core value of Buddhism. Guanzizai is a bodhisattva with both male and female identities, and innumerable manifestations, reputed to be responsive to the supplications of devotees. There is little knowledge of the origins of this bodhisattva. Some say he/she was a real person, perhaps even Maya, the Buddha's mother. Though this remains a matter of speculation, Guanzizai's infinite compassion towards sentient beings, and the great honour felt towards him/her, do suggest aspects of the Buddha's mother.

bodhisattva 菩萨

The word bodhisattva is usually explained as 'enlightened being'. It connotes seeking both nirvana for oneself and the liberation of others. Emphasis on this bodhisattva ideal is what makes Mahayana distinct from Hinayana, which favours the arhat ideal.

Line 2

practising the deep practice 行深

This refers to the Mahayana practice of 'deep wisdom', in which practitioners proceed until they reach the realm of awareness of Prajnaparamita, that is, enlightenment.

Line 3

looked upon 照见

This comprises two elements, first 'observe' and then 'see without obstruction'.

Five Skandhas 五蕴

The Sanskrit word *skandha* literally means 'trunk of a tree', and can be understood broadly as a verb, 'aggregate'. More specifically, skandhas are the paths, or methods, through which the human sensory and perceptual systems observe and experience both the internal mind and the external physical world. The Five Skandhas are the Skandha of Form, Skandha of Sensation, Skandha of Perception, Skandha of

Memory and Skandha of Consciousness. Form refers to the external world, including the physical body, and whatever we experience through the five senses. Sensation refers to how the sensory system experiences both the mind and the external world. Perception refers to integrated judgement and evaluation by the perceptual system, based on what has been taken in through sensation. Memory, or mental formation, can be understood as mental impressions or recollections of experiences, often concepts, obtained through the sensory and perceptual systems. Consciousness, connoting 'discrimination' or 'distinction', refers to how cognitive activities work in the intellectual system. The Five Skandhas represent five ways of experiencing the self and the world. Skandhas are not separate, but rather interconnected, because they do not stand still in the mind, but are in constant flux, like the ever-changing clouds in the sky.

Line 4

empty 空

Shunya in Sanskrit, meaning 'empty', refers to the lack of 'self-nature' of things and beings. It can also be viewed as a skandha. Emptiness is neither 'existence', nor 'non-existence'; neither 'being', nor 'non-being'. Emptiness defines the world, which, contrary to what the mind has imagined, is absent of intrinsic nature, and thus, illusory or 'empty' of inherent existence. Emptiness is also the awakened state of mind after it has obtained freedom from all attachments. Therefore, emptiness marks the drifting and ever-changing existence of skandhas, which lack self-nature, essence or permanence. The *Heart Sutra* describes the Five Skandhas as being 'empty of self-existence', implying that the Five Skandhas are attachments to be abandoned.

Following line 4, several Chinese translations interpolate the line 度一切苦厄, 'and was healed from all suffering'. Red Pine suggests this is because the Chinese translators noted the occurrence of this phrase towards the end of the sutra, in line 33, and decided a second occurrence near the beginning would help emphasise the point that emptiness is not nothingness but what liberates us from suffering (Red Pine, p. 69). However, no Sanskrit copy containing this line has been found.

Line 5
Shariputra 舍利子

Shariputra was one of the ten eminent disciples of the Buddha. He was known as 'foremost in wisdom' for his excellent understanding of the Buddhadharma. The other nine disciples were Katyayana (foremost in spreading the Dharma), Mogallana (foremost in possessing supernatural powers), Subhuti (foremost in realising emptiness), Purna (foremost in debating the Dharma), Mahakasyapa (foremost in asceticism), Aniruddha (foremost in attentiveness), Upali (foremost in upholding the precepts), Ananda (foremost in hearing the teachings of the Buddha) and Rahula (foremost in esoteric practices and desire for instruction of the Dharma).

Line 7
form is not separate from emptiness
色不异空

This line asserts the inseparability of form and emptiness, for, as isomorphic skandhas, they are like two sides of the same coin. Through drifting, form transforms into emptiness, and emptiness transforms into form, hence the turning and coursing of the form–emptiness wheel.

Line 9
The same holds for sensation and perception, memory and consciousness.
受想行识，亦复如是

Like the Skandha of Form, the other four skandhas remain adrift in the mind, following, respectively, the courses of the sensation–emptiness wheel, perception–emptiness wheel, memory–emptiness wheel and consciousness–emptiness wheel. The Five Skandhas represent five turning passages or drifting patterns of the mind. At the same time, the Five Skandhas drift between themselves, too, forming a new, whirling skandha of the mind, which is in constant transformation. The *Heart Sutra* is intended to undo the knot of the skandha of the mind, that is, to get rid of attachments, or suffering, of the mind, through turning the skandhas involved into emptiness, so that the mind will be liberated, and obtain freedom in emptiness.

Lines 10–11

all dharmas are defined by emptiness, not birth or destruction, purity or defilement, completeness or deficiency

诸法空相，不生不灭，不垢不净，不增不减

All dharmas (teachings of the Buddha) are defined by emptiness, because dharmas do not have inherent essence, or intrinsic nature. Dharmas and appearances, as provisional names, are also skandhas in a drifting state. They are all defined by emptiness.

Birth, destruction, purity, defilement, completeness and deficiency may have been considered characteristics of dharmas (the Five Skandhas included). However, under the law of dependent origination, all dharmas are said to be 'empty of self-existence'; and since the defining characteristic of all dharmas is emptiness, they can be neither born nor destroyed, neither purified nor defiled, neither complete nor deficient. All are but emptiness.

Lines 12–13

in emptiness there is no form, no sensation, no perception, no memory and no consciousness

空中无色，无受想行识

Chan (Zen) Master Nanyang Huizhong expressed it well by pointing out, 'dharmas are "empty" of an intrinsic nature, that is why they are defined by emptiness; form is void of an independent self, that is why it lacks existence; the mind is absent of substantiality, that is why there is no sensation, no perception, no memory and no consciousness.'[111] Of the 260 characters that make up the Chinese version of the *Heart Sutra*, the character *wu* (meaning 'nothing', or 'nothingness', often translated as 'no' in the context of *Heart Sutra*) appears 21 times. The concept of *wu* does not equate to nihilism. Rather, it refers to the domain of Suchness which, like a phantasm, is beyond the reach of sentient beings.

These lines claim that in emptiness there exist no such dharmas as the Five Skandhas, the Six Roots or the Six Dusts. To be more exact, *wu* does not imply that nothing exists at all, but that nothing created by the mind or languages can ever be identical to what exists out there in reality. As a result, existence and non-existence as signified by language or represented in the mind are only phantasms and illusions of reality. Hence, 'all dharmas are empty'.

Line 14
no eye, no ear, no nose, no tongue, no body and no mind 无眼耳鼻舌身意

Eye, ear, nose, tongue, body and mind are the six sensory organs of the body, namely, the Six Roots. They are the abodes of our sensory powers, providing six ways for us to experience and understand the world. Together with the Six Dusts, they form the Twelve Abodes. Bill Porter states:

---

111 *Translator's note:* Nanyang Huizhong (675–775) was a Chan monk of the Tang period (618–907). He was also the personal teacher of the Tang emperors Suzong and Daizong.

> In analysing the possible constituents of our world of awareness, early Buddhists did not limit themselves to the Five Skandhas but used several other conceptual frameworks. After the skandhas, the next most common analytical scheme involved a division of our awareness into the Twelve Abodes, or *ayatanas*. The word *ayatana* means 'resting place' and refers to the location in a home where a family kept its sacred fire. Thus, its use by Buddhists was meant to appeal to Brahmans and at the same time to redirect their spiritual endeavours to the sanctuary within us all. But instead of focusing on one *ayatana*, the Buddha directed his disciples to examine twelve locations, any one of which could be considered the abode of the sacred fire of our awareness.
>
> (p. 106)

Ayatana in this context is sometimes translated into 'entrance', for each 'abode' provides an 'entrance' to, or a starting point for, understanding the world.

Line 15
no shape, no sound, no smell, no taste, no feeling and no thought 无色声香味触法

Shape, sound, smell, taste, feeling and thought are the six domains in which our powers of sensation (the Six Roots) function, namely, the Six Dusts. The Six Dusts and the Six Roots, together, are called the Twelve Abodes. They are starting points where skandhas coalesce and emerge, as well as points of drifting or turning. Both the Five Skandhas and the Twelve Abodes are only provisional names for skandhas in their driftage, and are thus empty.

Line 16
no element of perception, from eye to conceptual consciousness
无眼界，乃至无意识界

The original line in Sanskrit literally means 'no element of eye through to no element of conceptual consciousness'. It denies the existence of the so-called Eighteen Realms, which represents another conceptual system, or, set of provisional names, to approach the world. The Eighteen Realms comprise the realms of the Six Roots, the Six Dusts and the Six Consciousnesses.

Lines 17–18
no causal link, from ignorance to old age and death, and no end of causal link, from ignorance to old age and death
无无明，亦无无明尽，乃至无老死，亦无老死尽

These lines discuss the 'transmigration' and 'extinction' of the Twelve Links of Dependent Arising. The Twelve Links of Dependent Arising are ignorance, *kamma* (volitional action); conditioned consciousness; name and form; the six sense organs; contact (sense impressions); sensation (feelings); desire (craving); attachment; existence (becoming); birth;

and *dukkha*, (old age and death, sorrow, lamentation, misery, grief and despair). To quote Master Hongyi:

> The Twelve Links of Dependent Arising explain the origins as well as sequence of suffering in the world. They expound the law of this world as well as the law of the world beyond by way of transmigration and extinction. What continues in the cycle of transmigration, from ignorance through to old age and death, reveals the law of this world; what returns to extinction, from 'end of ignorance' through to 'end of old age and death', reveals the law of the world beyond. In the eyes of those practising enlightenment, the law of this world is empty, hence, 'no ignorance', 'through to no old age and death'; the law of the world beyond is also empty, hence, 'no end of ignorance', 'through to no end of old age and death'.

The Twelve Links of Dependent Arising consist of twelve concepts, or twelve skandhas, to which Shakyamuni was awakened when he achieved enlightenment sitting under the bodhi tree. They are an assembly of skandhas, and each skandha is liable to get revealed in any drifting moment of transmigration and extinction. In fact, all causes and conditions are in constant flux, undergoing transmigration or extinction. In the mind realm, the becoming and cessation of causes and conditions are achieved through language rather than reality, for reality provides no entry into the mind unless through the passage of 'emptiness'.

Lines 19–20

no suffering, no source, no relief, no path; no knowledge, and no attainment, for nothing is to be attained 无苦集灭道，无智亦无得，以无所得故

Suffering, source, relief and path – the Four Noble Truths – were preached by the Buddha in his first sermon at Deer Park after his enlightenment. The proclamation of these four concepts, or, skandhas, is known as the 'first turning of the dharma wheel'. The Buddha's audience on that occasion were his first five disciples, Ashvajit, Vashpa, Mahanaman, Bhadrika and Kaundinya, who had accompanied Shakyamuni in his spiritual quest for enlightenment. Bill Porter points out:

> As with the previous analytical categories, the Four Truths address the same basic issue: the nature of our experience. The Five Skandhas explained it in terms of aspects or bodies, the Twelve Abodes explained it in terms of locations, the Eighteen Elements of Perception explained it in terms of components, and the Twelve Links of Dependent Origination explained it in terms of causal connections. It was this last insight that formed the basis of the Buddha's Enlightenment. Hence, it was only natural that he made this the subject of his first sermon. But instead of explaining the entire sequence of Dependent Origination, the Buddha taught his former colleagues a briefer version, and one that included a course of practice as well.
>
> (p. 122)

The 'briefer version' Bill Porter mentions is the Four Noble Truths.

Not only suffering, source, relief and path, but also knowledge and attainment – these are all skandhas, which, adrift, assume different provisional names for different signification. For instance, knowledge signifies prajna in flux, and attainment signifies the Buddha fruit, or the state of buddhahood. As 'imaginary oases' (provisional dwelling places) for skandhas on the road to buddhahood, knowledge and attainment are defined by emptiness; hence, 'no knowledge' and 'no attainment'. Master Hongyi explains, 'one should not cling to knowledge or attainment. The concept of "knowledge" is put forward to break delusions. Those attached to illusions will talk about "knowledge", but those awakened will not; thus it says there is "no knowledge". The concept of "attainment" is used to describe the future state of enlightenment. Upon attainment, one would realise that buddhahood lies in every being, no less in ordinary beings than in sacred beings; thus it says "no attainment"'.

Lines 21–4

Therefore, Shariputra, bodhisattvas take refuge in Prajnaparamita, and live without walls of the mind. Without walls of the mind and thus without fears, they see through delusions and finally nirvana.

菩提萨埵，依般若波罗蜜多故，心无挂碍，无挂碍故，无有恐怖，远离颠倒梦想，究竟涅槃。

'Walls of the mind' refers to attachments, which are obstructions to spiritual growth. 'Fears' connotes feelings of anxiety, concern, terror, and so on. To 'see through delusions' is to break the phantasm, and overcome the illusions of the mundane world in the mind. Nirvana is sometimes translated as 'extinction', or 'pass away', with the implication of drifting away from the sea of suffering and obtaining liberation. Walls, fears, delusions and nirvana are all skandhas coalesced in the mind. Skandhas are sometimes obstructed in their course, and other times dissolve in on-going drift.

Lines 25–8

All buddhas past, present and future also take refuge in Prajnaparamita and realise unexcelled, perfect enlightenment.

三世诸佛，依般若波罗蜜多故，得阿耨多罗三藐三菩提。

Buddhas of the three periods of time (past, present and future) represent all buddhas. They attain 'unexcelled, perfect enlightenment' simply by taking refuge in Prajnaparamita. 'Enlightenment' refers to the state of being awakened to true Suchness, having dispelled the darkness of ignorance and shadows of delusion. It is 'unexcelled' because it surpasses the understanding of those limited by concepts; it is 'perfect' because it is more complete than the understanding of those limited by reason.

Lines 29–33

You should therefore know the great mantra of Prajnaparamita, the mantra of great magic, the unexcelled mantra, the mantra equal to the unequalled, which heals all suffering and is true, not false

故知般若波罗蜜多，是大神咒，是大明咒，是无上咒，是无等等咒，能除一切苦，真实不虚。

Prajnaparamita, or 'perfection of wisdom', is a spiritual guide, or perfected way, leading to the Other Shore. A mantra is a sacred utterance, a numinous sound, a mystical formula of invocation or incantation, which is believed by practitioners to have magical or spiritual powers. Sometimes, it has no semantic meaning whatsoever; at other times it may take the form of a phrase, and is called *dharani*. In Sanskrit, the word *mantra* has an additional meaning of 'refuge' or 'protector', implying that it provides a provisional dwelling place for numinous sounds, or an energy field where magical powers gather. Ultimately, a mantra is magical language, a path 'identified' or established by early sages leading to the mind, reality and existence. It is the path leading to Prajnaparamita; it also represents the life rhythm of Prajnaparamita, adrift and wandering. Prajnaparamita has no end in its existence other than staying adrift with a dynamic life rhythm. Chanting a mantra reveals the chanter's faith in the magical power of language.

Master Hongyi says:

> A mantra is mystical beyond understanding and has great magical power. By claiming Prajnaparamita to be 'the great mantra of Prajnaparamita', the sutra emphasises its magical effectiveness and efficiency in liberating the mind, and in overcoming suffering. It is called 'the mantra of great magic', because it can dispel the darkness of ignorance and shadow of delusion; 'the unexcelled mantra', because it brings causal practices to completion with nothing left to be added; 'the mantra equal to the unequalled', because it fulfils the merits of nirvana and achieves unsurpassed enlightenment. Being 'not false' tells about the nature of prajna, and 'healing all suffering' tells about the function of prajna.

Lines 34–5
the mantra in Prajnaparamita spoken thus, 'Gate gate, paragate, parasangate, bodhi svaha'

故说般若波罗蜜多咒，即说咒曰：揭谛揭谛，波罗揭谛，波罗僧揭谛，菩提萨婆诃。

According to Bill Porter:

> The operative term here is 'in'. This mantra is in Prajnaparamita because it is her womb, which she creates through its sound and which we enter

through sympathetic harmonics when we chant it. Some mothers sing lullabies. Prajnaparamita sings this mantra. The reason Avalokiteshvara knows this mantra is that he is a subsequent incarnation of Maya, the mother of Shakyamuni, and thus a manifestation of Prajnaparamita, the Mother of All Buddhas. In Vajrayana Buddhism, Avalokiteshvara is also known as the *vidya-adhipati,* 'bestower of spells'.

(p. 154–5)

Gate means 'arrive'; *para* means 'the Other Shore', or 'transcend'; *san* means 'completely'; 'bodhi' means 'awakening' or 'enlightenment'; *svaha* means 'instantly'.

Like spring winds blowing and bringing life back to the land, the chanting of mantras liberates lives from the sea of suffering, ferrying them to the Other Shore where there is no obstruction, but instead perfect freedom. Therefore, all mantras can be taken as mantras of Prajnaparamita. In the end, all mantras will become one, and this one mantra is also capable of being transformed into numerous mantras, just as all skandhas can coalesce into one skandha in the realm of language, and that one skandha is capable of being transformed into numerous skandhas. Mantras and skandhas undergo constant division and coalescence; they either get unfolded through provisional existence, or transformed as a result of drifting. Prajnaparamita is both a mantra and a skandha; it is the blissful state achieved from a harmony between the two.

About the Author

Li Sen was born in Yunnan Province, China, in 1966. He is currently professor of Literary Criticism at Yunnan University, and was the former dean of the School of Chinese Language and Literature there. He concurrently holds the following academic titles and positions: chairman of the Research Centre for Chinese Contemporary Art and Literature; member of the National Advisory Committee on Teaching Artistic Theory in Higher Education, under the Ministry of Education; editor-in-chief of *New Poetry Magazine* (Chinese); and member of the 'Them' school of poets, a well-known poetry school founded in 1984 in mainland China.

Professor Li has published more than ten books, both monographs and edited collections, and more than four hundred shorter pieces, both academic papers and creative writing.

About the Translator

Deng Zhihui is currently professor of Translation Studies at Sun Yat-sen University in China. Her research interests include the translation process and translation of classical Chinese philosophy. As an experienced translator and interpreter, she was Grand Champion of the 'English World Cup' National Translation Competition in 2014.

If you enjoyed this book,

please visit our website

www.heartspacepublications.com

for many other books on wellness.

www.ingramcontent.com/pod-product-compliance
Lightning Source LLC
Chambersburg PA
CBHW070249010526
44107CB00056B/2391